The Sociology of Art

Jean Duvignaud

The
Sociology of Art

Translated from the French
by Timothy Wilson

Icon Editions
Harper & Row, Publishers
New York, Evanston, San Francisco, London

First published under the title *Sociologie de l'Art* by Presses Universitaires de France 1967.
Copyright © Presses Universitaires de France 1967.

FIRST U.S. EDITION

STANDARD BOOK NUMBER: 06-43201-3 (cloth); 06-430035-8 (paper)

LIBRARY OF CONGRESS CATALOG CARD NUMBER: 72-14012

Contents

Foreword

Duvignaud's Wager: Toward a Modern Sociology of Art

Shortly before he died Herbert Read wrote, more in sorrow than in anger, that 'art criticism, with notable exceptions in our time such as the work of the Marxist critic, Georg Lukács, has made little attempt to deal with art as a social phenomenon, as a positive factor in the immediate resolution of the problems of contemporary society'.[1] He might have been reassured to some extent if he had come into close contact with the writings of the French sociologist and author Jean Duvignaud, whose book *The Sociology of Art* is now being made available in English.

Jean Duvignaud, though relatively little known in this country outside sociological circles familiar with his 'report from a North African Village', *Change at Shebika*, is a prolific writer now in his early fifties who occupies a Chair at the University of Orléans. Apart from novels, essays on Planchon, Büchner and Arland, he has published works of general sociology, including editions of Durkheim and Gurvitch, as well as the massive *Sociologie du théâtre* (Paris, 1965), the first of a triptych of studies devoted to the sociology of drama. He is therefore particularly well qualified to turn his attention in this book to wider aspects of the sociology of art, a subject which has attracted some of the finest critical minds of the century, notably, Benjamin, Sartre and Lukács. It soon becomes evident to the reader of this book, indeed, that these are the sort of writers in whose company Duvignaud fits best. Although not committed to any clearly identifiable ideological position – he probably refers as frequently to the German idealist philosopher

Wilhelm Dilthey as he does to Karl Marx – he is not much interested either in pragmatic, empirical sociology of art as pursued, for example, at the Institute of Bordeaux under Robert Escarpit, or at Richard Hoggart's Birmingham Centre for Contemporary Cultural Studies. He proposes instead a theoretical structure based on a personal conception of the imaginative function. Personal as it is, though, it conforms with a widely-held concern for this sort of approach in France, where expectations of art are changing, and with them a new type of criticism is being sought for, such as that offered in philosophy and literature by Michel Foucault and Roland Barthes.

What Jean-Paul Sartre did for the psycho-philosophical study of the imaginative function as early as 1940 in his book *L'Imaginaire*, Duvignaud seems now to have achieved on the sociological side. Not that Duvignaud is exactly an orthodox, run-of-the-mill sociologist. His book on Shebika blandly asserts that if Balzac and Dickens were alive today they would be sociologists, and the inverse equally applies. *Change at Shebika* has been described by Cecil Hourani as a *theatrical* work in which sociology 'reveals its full capacities not merely to study men, but also to change them'.[2] The book, originally published in French in 1968 after Duvignaud had taught for a period at Tunis University, undoubtedly made a distinct impact on the Tunisians, both on the villagers in whose midst Duvignaud and his colleagues worked, and on the westernized intellectuals who govern them. As far as one can tell the contact was a fruitful one, not only for them but also for him, since it appears to have convinced him of the need for micro-societies to achieve social independence in order that the social evils of both East and West can be avoided. 'As a French intellectual of the left', writes Hourani, 'Duvignaud can accept neither the myth of liberal capitalist society in which finally the individual loses all sense of community, and in which his search for private self-realization and personal happiness ends in complete egoism or in despair; nor the myth of orthodox Communism that a monolithic State or a party can create a free society.' There is little hint of all this in *The Sociology of Art*, which comes apparently from an earlier and less committed Duvignaud; none the less, as his admiration for Oscar Lewis reveals, he offers Shebika a similar 'act of total social imagination', stressing the element of invention – sociology is on a par with literature in such 'Utopian reconstructions', in the *wager* on a backward village's collective existence. This dedication to *imaginative* models of sociological description and analysis runs right through Duvignaud's work. An earlier essay, significantly entitled 'To Enter the Twentieth Century',[3] ends with a section entitled 'Courage and the Imagination'. Similarly, his *Introduction to Sociology* proposes that the discipline should concern itself less with a Comteian analysis of institutions than with the study of social change, with *dynamics* rather than *statics*. Sociology, he argues, once again consciously echoing Sartre, is a humanism: 'Mankind, in the eyes of the sociologist, is an infinite experience perpetually to be mastered.'[4] Likewise his *Sociology of Theatre* sees the stage as a freer of collective tensions, a permanent revolt against all established orders, and the collected essays issued under the title *Spectacle et Société* follow this up by stressing the relation between a living aesthetic and social structures, in particular between the proscenium arch and the society whose conflicts it allows harmlessly to be sublimated. 'A social system,' he concludes, 'never replaces another without dramatizing the classifications and myths of its predecessor, as if to grant it a last image of itself, to make permanent its survival on another plane, and to revel in its passing away.'[5] But this is always after, or instead of, revolutions; revolutionary movements, says Duvignaud, have no theatre other than tiresome propaganda because, in so far as they represent social crises, they themselves constitute dramatizations of the historical process.

It's easy to perceive from the present book those whom he

feels closest to in his asseveration that 'societies by definition never attain a final form'. Lévi-Strauss is already well-known in this country, Blanchot and Francastel less so; but possibly the most marked influence is Edgar Morin, and in particular his book *Le Cinéma ou l'homme imaginaire*. In this book, Morin establishes early on some important distinctions between art forms which, although they bear a close aesthetic relationship to each other, diverge sociologically in significant ways. The Lied, for example, is like the song in form, but it differs from it in being the product of a special social system, characterized by after-dinner amateur musical entertainments performed by accomplished but otherwise socially unproductive young ladies. Likewise the short story, imposed by the readership of mass-circulation magazines, differs from the folk-tale, the product of a very different socio-economic climate; and a similar distinction can be established between grand opera and musical comedy spectaculars, the one created largely by and for a bourgeois élite, the other of lower middle-class mass origins, but both appealing, like the Lieder recital, to an ever more sophisticated and moneyed public as the passage of time imperceptibly converts into a form of high culture what was originally devised as entertainment. It is striking, however, that few short-story magazines now survive, that few Lieder, or operas on a large scale, are written any longer, and that even the musical is being transformed out of all recognition as the Rock happening increasingly elbows it out of the arena, where newly constituted audiences pay for a tune rather different from the one their parents' pipers were called upon to play.

These considerations lead Morin naturally to see the cinema in the context of a similar socio-cultural nexus of forces. He draws attention to the crucial fact that 'those who brought about the metamorphosis of the cinematograph into the cinema were not worthy professionals, chartered thinkers or eminent artists, but do-it-yourself self-taught men, professional failures, frauds, mountebanks . . .'[6] These were the people who made possible the projection and objectification of our dreams in the shape of films produced industrially and consumed collectively, since mankind's reality is, as Gorki saw, always semi-imaginary. It is up to the sociologist of the cinema to reintegrate the fictive in man's consciousness of reality. Morin thus sees the cinema – like other art forms – as being intimately dependent upon, as well as influenced and affected by, its social context; and it is clearly his perception of the dynamic nature of this relationship which endears his vision to Duvignaud. It is only after that perception has been established that the work of art can be considered, appreciated and evaluated *outside* that context; but this *intrinsic* estimation is something which we shall find the sociology of art cannot perhaps so easily handle or even account for.

Nevertheless, Morin's account of the sociology of the 'seventh art' can help us situate accurately what Duvignaud is attempting in the present work: nothing less than a sketch or prolegomenon to a sociology of the *imaginative function itself*. He draws our attention early on to his conviction that 'the imagination is much more than the imaginary' since 'it embraces the entire existence of man – for we do not only respond with feeling or admiration, but participate, through the symbols offered by a work of the imagination, in a *potential society which lies beyond our grasp*' (p. 20, my italics). It is here that Duvignaud most clearly transcends traditional sociologies of art. The world is eternally being made, it constitutes a perpetual *becoming*, and the role of the imaginative function in man is of crucial, indeed cardinal importance in this 'permanent revolution' about which we nowadays tend to hear so much. But nearly always in monotonously narrow political terms, neo-Marxist or crypto-Fascist. Duvignaud, very much in this respect the heir to the essential Surrealism shorn of the cant and ballyhoo which tended to cloud perception of it in the thirties, would agree with Walter Benjamin's famous observation that Fascism aestheticizes politics while Communism politicizes art, and reject both alternatives. He suggests as much in his introductory remarks on religious and political definitions of art, both of which he finds unduly restrictive. His instinct inclines him towards a more humanistic view of a world in which, as we shall see, societies are never 'completed', but remain in a state of perpetual dynamic evolution; and it is here, as André Breton and his circle rightly perceived, that the imagination has the principal role to play. 'There is room,' Duvignaud modestly suggests, 'for a sociology of art whose starting point is both a real experience of creativity and an equally dynamic experience of actual life within society. The task of such a sociology of art would be to find, without being dogmatic or pedantic, the extent to which the imaginary is rooted in collective life' (p. 21). But we should not be misled by his demure fondness for the rhetorical question into underestimating the radical nature of his approach to the sociology of art, or its originality. In his first chapter he clears away 'confusions' of an aesthetic and ideological nature which have tended to hinder or obstruct the development of a sociology of the imaginative function. Effectively, if unobtrusively, he then demolishes much that passes for the sociology of art; 'should it not', he wonders in one of his characteristic tones of voice, 'have a keen interest in questioning pre-conceived ideas about the unity of an era in order to try to perceive any divergencies of language and intentions, especially when modern criticism explains everything in abstract terms of harmony or of coherent systems?' In case we miss who is being politely but firmly taken to task in this rhetorical question, he comes out in the open a few pages further on:

We shall not discuss the interpretations put on the novel by Hegel or by Lukács, because it seems to us that the great proliferation of this type of imagined experience in prose form owes its importance, not to the momentary situation of a class, but to the discovery, which remained unresolved, of the existence of a tension between groups in the whole of a society. *Moll Flanders*, *Lady Roxana*, *Le Paysan parvenu*, *Marianne*, Julien Sorel and Rastignac do not reflect a determination to be 'bourgeois'; they are the result of a question posed by the writer concerning the multiplicity of possibilities available in a society whose organization remains 'mysterious' according to some, and 'anarchic' according to others . . . The determination, the ambition to 'get to the top', the desire for power, the Caesarism or the 'opportunism' of the heroes of the European novel, surely all these are questions posed by the novelist about the opportunities for effective action available to a man in society around him? The ways and means of freedom, surely, are symbolized in this attempt by a character to master society?

Yes, it's a brand of Marxist sociology of art that he's attacking, isn't it? Not because he disagrees with its political intention, but because he can't accept the rigidity of its analyses when applied to the subject under discussion. Great as is his respect for Lukács, made clear in Chapter 2, he is lucid about the limitations of his predecessor's theory of art, and in particular the way it fails to account meaningfully for contemporary art forms, i.e. precisely those that are in a state of *becoming* rather than of having *become*. In taking Lukács to task for 'the inadequacies or banalities of the kind which occur when he writes about Joyce or Beckett', Duvignaud is being fully consistent with his own view of artistic creation as a 'mirror or a schema of a freedom which seeks through (or in spite of) old determinisms to suggest new relationships between men' (pp. 89–90).

It's within the context of this general theory that the value of his particular and individual insights can best be judged. He is very perceptive, here and in *Spectacle et Société*, about Shakespeare's attitude to kingship, not so much the *conscious* idea the playwright had of royalty (to the extent that this can be ascertained from the chronicle plays), as the sociologically-conditioned *instinct* that the death and coronation of kings is an 'infernal cycle' since 'power can never be permanently established' (p. 87). Or, speaking of classical tragedy, he suggests that 'those who wish to reduce the theatre to a piece of folk-lore or a simple reflection of social life fail to take account of the existence of an individual protagonist or hero who is tormented and ridiculed because he has transgressed commonly-held taboos'.[7] Duvignaud's approach can, in fact, be applied on numerous levels. His method is exciting because it is continually suggestive in an indirect sort of way. Moving nearer to our own times, he has some very pertinent things to say about Flaubert, or about the well-worn topic of the impact of film and television media on our view of ourselves. Extending Benjamin's meditations on 'The Work of Art in the Age of Mechanical Reproduction',[8] Duvignaud shows how in the last couple of decades 'the detailed presentation of living history has actually become a factor in the way history is perceived, and this in turn implies an intense dramatization of man's life in the universe' (p. 132). The cinema, he goes on, has revolutionized the contemporary arts in several ways. In so far as it makes explicit what had previously been only implicit in human relationships (the sort of thing Chekhov sought with infinite pains to express in the theatre), it transforms into spectacle, overt representation, precisely those hitherto secret and inarticulate elements of everyday life. Or again, in so far as it is an art of collage by virtue of the technique of montage which Morin rightly sees as one of the most important discoveries in the whole history of the imagination, the film's techniques of discontinuity have not failed to influence the novel, and Butor's *Mobile* is cited as an example of this.

It's evident, therefore, why this book (which deals, of course, with art in general and not merely with painting) is of such importance in the field to which it claims to be only an introduction. It is, as I have shown, a great deal more than that: at once a critique and an extension of previous theories, some masterly like those of Sartre, Lukács and Benjamin, others more questionable, like Ernst Fischer's *The Necessity of Art* (Penguin Books) or Lucien Goldmann's *Pour une sociologie du roman* (Paris, 1964). Herbert Read is the nearest we Anglo-Saxons come to such an ambitious attempt at evolving a general theory of the relationship between art and society.[9] Normally we over here would agree with René Wellek that if 'literature occurs only in a social context, as part of a culture, in a milieu' it none the less seems to be the case that the relationships are 'devious and oblique';[10] it's easy to collect data about the interaction between art and society, less easy to interpret them. To some extent Duvignaud transcends this whole argument about ways and means which exercises British critics like Hoggart, Bradbury and Holloway.[11] On the other hand, because he is free of the dogmatism of some Marxist critics he does not fail to come to grips with the problem of artistic excellence. In a recent television series, John Berger became dangerously reductive about the relationship between the European tradition of easel painting and the societies that gave rise to this unique form of artistic activity. 'This is a portrait,' he said of Holbein's *The Ambassadors*, 'of two men convinced that the world is there to furnish their residence in it';[12] and even more naïve is his comment on Gainsborough's superb study of figures in a landscape called – for its sins perhaps, in order that Berger may ridicule the sitters – 'Mr and Mrs Andrews'. Turning to the country scene behind and to the right of the subjects, Berger remarks: 'Look at their expressions, their gestures. Their attitude is visible. One can imagine on the tree behind them the notice: "Trespassers will be prosecuted." ' This might well be true of any third-rate wooden commissioned portrait of which, as Berger rightly says, hundreds of thousands were painted at the time, but does it touch Gainsborough, or even begin to come to grips with what is uniquely excellent in his art? Ernst Fischer is less doctrinaire, but even he cannot easily reconcile his conviction that Mozart is one of the world's greatest composers with the disturbingly evident fact that in any society short of the Communist utopia whose birth we are still awaiting 'the Viennese operetta would triumph over him in almost any plebiscite' (p. 209).

Is it really fair to maintain, as Fischer does, that 'the late bourgeois world has a profound distaste for any application of sociology to the arts' (p. 180)? Does this not rather depend on *what* sociology, and what kind of application? The naïve way Goldmann, for example, parallels his over-simplified view of twentieth-century economic history with an almost equally simplistic account of the development of the French novel in the same period[13] is not likely to do credit to any 'application of sociology to the arts', Marxist or otherwise. It is true, of course, that the defects of such approaches are due less to their being Marxist, than to their being muddled or mechanical in their application of Marxist techniques of analysis: after all, Marx himself said 'je ne suis pas marxiste' when he perceived what some of his disciples were capable of. Obviously, if the sociology of art tries to link artistic manifestations up too closely – or too rigidly – with class systems, economic developments or social structures of a given time and place, it will tend to fail. But if it is the sociological analysis of the role and function of the *imaginative faculty* at any given time or place – something for which Jean Duvignaud, in this seminal book, sketches a general theory – it has every chance of being a great deal more effective. That way it becomes 'a wager on the capacity of human beings to invent new relationships and to experience hitherto unknown emotions . . . for we are as much what we have been as what we are able to imagine' (pp. 143–5). This is the full dimension of Duvignaud's wager, and the measure of his confidence and of his hopes for mankind. Profoundly pessimistic towards the end of his life, Herbert Read saw the main function of art as being to 'reconcile man to his destiny, which is death'. I fancy that Duvignaud would put it rather differently, and claim that the role of art, as an aspect of a wider imaginative function, is to *connect* man with his destiny, which is life.

JOHN FLETCHER

Introduction

Toward a Sociology of Artistic Expression*

A famous book on art should bear this annotation: 'The great red and blue mask of the New Hebrides is not gazing up at God in the depths of the sky. The wild eyes of Kalakh's *Mona Lisa* are not riveted on the shadowy gods of Assur. The *Naked Eve* of Dürer or Cranach does not turn her face towards the Great Judge beyond the skies for the first time in Europe with eyes of proud passion. It is we for whom these are waiting. It is *we* who give them form . . .'

'We' – what does this mean? Not, certainly, 'man', with or without a capital 'm', invested with some great 'destiny' as conceived by humanism. This 'we' refers to us in our pulsing, restless, reckless world. To whom else does Hamlet speak if not to those who, with him, can expose the emptiness of the universe? I have seen Ruhr miners listening to the long lament of Antigone in a kind of holy silence and with an intensity comparable to that expressed by Hölderlin. What can these miners possibly have in common with the little barbarian princess condemned to death for having carried out a rite which was already obsolete when Sophocles dramatized the story? Yet they did feel involved.

This is the crux. We may detach ourselves from the specifically religious and politics tend to annoy us, but Cézanne's *La Montagne Sainte-Victoire* or a character like Julien Sorel persistently demand our complete involvement. It is *we* who give Alyosha Karamazov that power to go to

* This outline of a sociology of art will be more fully developed in the author's *Sociologie de l'imaginaire*.

the farthest limits of human experience, as it was the little nation of olive eaters and gossips who strengthened the determination of Orestes.

'We' . . . And yet Hamlet is right to be astonished when he greets the players who are to help him trap the King:

> . . . Now I am alone.
> O, what a rogue and peasant slave am I!
> Is it not monstrous that this player here,
> But in a fiction, in a dream of passion,
> Could force his soul so to his own conceit
> That from her working all his visage wann'd;
> Tears in his eyes, distraction in's aspect,
> A broken voice, and his whole function suiting
> With forms to his conceit? And all for nothing!
> For Hecuba!
> What's Hecuba to him, or he to Hecuba,
> That he should weep for her?   (*Hamlet*, II, ii)

He weeps for her as we do, a figment of the imagination. Though unreal, she affects us more than our own flesh and blood; she exerts more influence over us than the forces at work in the universe.'For Hecuba! . . .' But in the imaginary experience which artistic creation offers us, everything is 'for Hecuba'.

A painted mask of Mali has no more objective reality than the characters in Stendhal's novels. No woman ever looked like the *Eve* at Autun, threading her way through the floating leaves. No conqueror ever realized his ignominy with the acuteness of Shakespeare's *Richard III*. For someone concerned with measuring the exact correlation between what actually is and its verbal description, such images might appear frivolous, more or less cleverly fabricated illusions. But who, without appearing foolish, will assume that?

According to Kant, we become involved in artistic creation the moment we think about the impact of a particular work. If someone standing in front of Rousseau's *Joueuse de flûte* shrugs his shoulders and laughs, we feel deeply offended: we have been insulted. It is as if our awareness of the work includes an unformulated judgement, as if that work gives us a glimpse of some idea which might reveal and clarify the whole meaning of our human existence. That idea can never be put into words, but it still remains, uniquely ours.

Does it need to be pointed out that with this view Kant destroyed the very aesthetic theory he claims to be formulating? No doubt before him, when people were more concerned with the actual finished work of art and its effect, judgement and taste were considered synonymous in evaluating the artist and his work, even if the work was deemed 'the work of the devil', or unconsciously contradicted the norms which were imposed on it. Yet because he was inquiring into the origins of that mysterious influence exerted by what he calls, with despairing naïvety, 'the beautiful', Kant discovered that art was deeply rooted in life itself. And, later, the psychology of the creative process gradually superseded judgements based on the success and the 'achievement' of a work of art, which is what aesthetics had been reduced to. However, some concepts can illuminate others and in this case, although Kant was trying to establish aesthetic criteria, he unexpectedly discovered – and enabled his successors to discover it more quickly than they otherwise would have done – the idea of conscious artistic creation.

It is crucial to realize that the work of art draws on infinitely more than material existence. In this context a psychological approach is inadequate. More precisely, the psychology of art only sketches in an outline which, since by itself it is incomplete, must be given real form by being set within a much wider context. The work of art creates anew behind us an order which brings together the separated fragments of mankind. And this order is based, not on a vague and absurd idea of man, but on the realization of that involvement and communication in which our freedom finds its true expression.

In turn, when the artist creates his work, he seems to incorporate into it an invisible community, the spirit of a society in which the social substance, the 'manna' which holds the secret of our future existence, is crystallized. Perhaps he can do this because we will never know absolute joy.

This is possibly the reason why a number of artists tend either to define art in religious terms or to seek some political commitment for themselves. Yet to define artistic experience in religious terms is to cling to the dream of close fellowship which smaller groups or sects offer their members, and this is to give 'the primitive tribe' an importance and a relevance which in reality it never had, except in the eyes of the first sociologists.

A similar kind of nostalgia is revealed in the attempt to reconcile art and humanity through political involvement, whether in revolution or a totalitarian state. As we know, the misunderstandings and anguish which ensue when the artist identifies himself with such collective endeavours, always inevitably restricted once the energies become institutionalized, are fatal to the creative imagination.

The imagination, therefore, is much more than the imaginary. It embraces the entire existence of man. For we do not only respond with feeling or admiration, but participate, through the symbols offered by a work of the imagination, in a potential society which lies beyond our grasp.

Few attempts have been made to deal with these problems. Those who have studied artistic expression have been more anxious to look for precepts, to establish norms, to repeat patterns, to measure effects, than to understand and really examine the total dimension which the imagined experience encompasses. Or else they have tried to associate the images and forms of the imagination with actual facts or real events. As though it was not a case of two parallel and often dissimilar levels! Who would have the audacity to attempt to trace the connection between Beethoven's last piano compositions or Rimbaud's *Les Illuminations* and their creators' everyday existence, against which these works justifiably protest?

Others have sought to make works of art reveal what their authors might have intended to say or conceal, and explain them in terms of utterly alien arguments. Following this method psychological analysis does no more than read between the lines or seize on ambiguities. But the work of art says no more than what it is in itself – and what we give it. What is this arrangement of symbols but a stimulus to direct us to the objects symbolized which, in themselves, have meaning for us. Only a permanent meaning, beyond our immediate awareness, will suffice. So much for works of art which satisfy at first reading and fall an easy prey to criticism!

That 'we' returns . . . There is such a thing as a sociology of art, but it has a bad name – and rightly so. Among all those who have dealt with artistic experience, who has ever defended the inexhaustible originality of the imagination? Who has understood the real task of sociology, which is not to regard the individual merely as a part of collective life but to understand him in his unique, irreducible individuality? If that mistaken attitude prevails, it reduces artistic creation to a series of events reconstructed with variable success from reality, in the same way that archaeologists in the past reconstructed ruins. People frequently forget that sociology should never speak of society as petrified or static, but rather should see it as a movement of collective, dynamic creativity which nothing can halt because, by definition, societies never attain a final form.

Once these confusions are resolved, there is room for a sociology of art whose starting point is both a real experience of creativity and an equally dynamic experience of actual life within society. The task of such a sociology of art would be to find, without being dogmatic or pedantic, the extent to which the imaginary is rooted in collective life.

Undertaken in this way, a sociology of art would clarify art even to the artist, and would give as comprehensive a meaning as is possible to the search for new forms.

However, before taking the first necessarily tentative steps in such a study, we ought to resolve some of the aesthetic and ideological confusions which for too long now have hindered the development of an authentic sociology of the imagination.

1 The Myths of Aesthetic Theory

If it is going to establish a method and a goal for itself, a modern sociology of artistic expression must abandon certain premises, or, at least, certain of the more or less prominent myths which still encumber it. Anyone wanting to study the nature of artistic creation, in so far as it springs from collective life, must seriously question these theories if he is to avoid becoming enclosed within the narrow concepts of an ideology, which *per se* tends to distort experience by reducing it to an isolated aspect, which is then given an arbitrary, over-exaggerated value.

Undoubtedly the first of these myths is the assumption that there is *an essence of art*. According to this, the infinite variety of human expression must be ascribed either to some absolute mental process transcending all particular manifestations, or to an 'essence' set apart from all earthly reality in the realm of pure ideas.

This 'platonism' is not the exclusive prerogative of idealists or ontologists. Surprisingly, one finds traces of it in critical analysis where it takes the form of an unstated presupposition which permeates every critical statement and judgement. Even the man in the street, judging by surveys, apparently holds the same opinion.* Both in conversation and in criticism as penetrating as that of Ruskin or Wölfflin, we continually come across the idea of artistic expression as

---

* Popular opinion declares what one wants it to reveal and its 'spontaneous' reactions express the values spread by education, advertising, and the radio, rather than any real set of values or expectations.

a 'self-contained entity', as though it was a unique source of inspiration for a great many forms of activity.

Although there are obviously other sources, perhaps the man most responsible for this platonic concept is the German aesthetician Johann Winckelmann. In his *History of Ancient Art* (1764), Winckelmann draws an unexpected conclusion from the discovery of Herculaneum in 1738 and then of Pompeii in 1748. Instead of defining art as an 'imitation of nature',* he describes it as the empirical realization, always imperfect of course, of an ideal beauty – a view similar to that which subsequently inspired David and Ingres, Goethe and Hölderlin. While Winckelmann's other theories (on balanced harmony, the superiority of pure form, and so on) have long been forgotten, this hypothesis of his has become commonplace in intellectual circles, and has been used, long after its historical origin has been forgotten, at all levels of critical theory and analysis.

This belief, it appears, owes its origin to the special meaning, totally unrelated to the real situation of the artist, of the '*idiotismes*' mentioned by Diderot in *Le Neveu de Rameau*. Popular sociology, based on the unthinking opinions of groups or individuals (which try to incorporate the indefinable into patently contrived general norms) cannot understand artistic creation except in terms of some kind of magical process. In other words, because the artist is by nature a radically unconventional person, he is considered to live on an altogether higher plane of reality, alien to the everyday life of society which then attempts to reconcile his peculiarities by attributing them to an 'essence'. Obviously the artist has nothing to lose by accepting this image of himself which rehabilitates him in the eyes of society (which *can* also protest against the artist's extravagant individualism); it acts as an excuse for the liberties he takes and justifies the

* He was attacking another myth – that of art being subservient to nature or to reality (the ideology which lay behind French neo-classicism), which we shall discuss later.

24

artist for being what he is, since his peculiarities are compensated for by his possession of a transcendent, intangible power.

The damage caused by this myth, and the absurdities to which it has led, can never be fully calculated. Instead of basing their analysis on real meanings and the relationship of these to human experience, critics have relied on the concept of an 'essence' of art to solve a problem which otherwise would become increasingly more difficult, requiring new working hypotheses, still unformulated and, through lack of effort, never confronted.

For a long time this theory belonged exclusively to very narrow artistic groups and creative élites, but in the last century it changed its social sphere and spread to the middle classes whose basic education through school and art galleries, popular books and more recently radio, films and television, has been dominated by the idea of 'beauty' or the 'possibility of beauty's existence'. Paradoxically this belief has even been strengthened by the emergence of various techniques of reproduction which have made the world's art accessible to everyone. And those who suddenly feel for reasons of social prestige that they ought to discuss art, but who out of ignorance have to rely on popularizers, also further extend the strange notion that there is an absolute beauty from which everyone can receive grace.

The second of these aesthetic myths which impede the development of an authentic sociology of art is expressed almost daily in theories, normally unfounded, on *the primitive origins of art*.

In fact, this so-called explanation is nothing but a disguised version of the first because, like that, it sets out to separate artistic expression from real experience, by associating the former with a privileged kind of existence, pure and detached from all actuality. One can see this from the number of books on painting, the theatre, architecture, poetry, music or literature which attempt to trace contemporary artistic forms back to the 'primitive' – all the more mysterious, of course, because we know so little about it.

There exist, besides, many popular books with titles such as 'The Origin of Painting', 'Music, from its Origins to Today' or even 'From Primitive Theatre to Shakespeare'. This fashion (or mania) for explaining things by their distant origin in the simplicity of primitive eras surely dates from the time when Europeans started to discover ancient ruins. But it was during the last century that this idea was really encouraged – by the popularization of prehistory and archaeological finds, by the increasingly frequent discovery of 'primitive' man and of unrecorded 'civilizations'.* Even today, the wall paintings of Altamira are frequently cited as the precursors of modern painting.†

Properly understood, this theory rests on a vision of man as unique and universal, whose history ('the story of mankind') has only a weak sense of continuity. It is thus possible to relate the earliest forms of human creativity to the most modern kinds of expression. Nietzsche's ideas on the 'birth of tragedy' are one of the most articulate (and poetic) versions of this nostalgia for the past, which links actual artistic creation to a creativity 'before civilization', outside history.

Who can fail to see what lies behind this belief? Surely the desire to anchor problems, which are essentially modern, in pre-history and primitive simplicity, thereby giving them

* A revival of classical forms by European artists in the sixteenth and seventeenth centuries grew out of a different attitude; namely, the search for already existing models, the adaptation of which would allow the artist to innovate and, at the same time, would protect him from the dangers of new myths. For Racine, Greek themes are a pretext; for Hölderlin, they are a form of nostalgia.

† This is the result of presenting, in a simplified form, authentic scientific discoveries which in themselves are really very complex; but the impact of popular science is only greater than that of science itself, particularly nowadays, because of the mass media which leaves nothing untouched.

the kind of nobility normally attached to mythical themes. In fact, this only reveals our own struggle against decline and decadence,[1] the effort, like Faust's in his love for Margaret, to perpetuate youth?[2]

In fact, this theory which exalts the origin of things is associated with the 'evolutionism' or 'historicism' which, from Spencer to Comte, Durkheim, and Bergson (without mentioning the moderns), asserted the continuous progress of man from the earliest times up to the present day.

This evolutionary theory (closely connected with the growth of natural sciences, paleontology and physiology) takes for granted three overlapping assumptions, all equally unfounded. These three propositions are as follows: that simplicity and primitiveness merge the closer one gets to the origins of man; that the complexity of present-day conditions results from a progressive combination of simple elements already present at the beginning of human history; and that, in spite of the disruptions which have occurred, the evolution of creative activity is continuous. According to these, therefore, the complexity of modern life can be understood in relation to the simplicity of primitive societies.[3]

How many theories about art have avoided these assumptions? Yet there is no real evidence that ancient, primitive societies were any closer to nature and simplicity. In fact, modern anthropology shows us that archaic classifications are no less complex than those of contemporary societies. Also, merely by recombining simple elements we cannot reconstruct the complex 'whole' of any ancient society, separated as it is from subsequent societies by a great gap in time. To try to absorb radically different societies into some improbable theory of history is to surely obliterate the very characteristics which give these societies their individuality? It is, finally, doubtful whether one can prove any real continuity between different societies which seem foreign to us now on account of their very antiquity. And it is highly unlikely that we will ever succeed in projecting ourselves to the other end of history which, after all, remains ill-defined and only an extension of our present time.

In art itself, it is only recently that painters like Picasso, Juan Gris or Atlan have begun to use symbols taken from the language of races which belong to a pre-historical era and which are supposedly 'archaic'. As André Malraux said in *The Voices of Silence*: 'we have *learnt* to see the primitive world which we have always been looking at'. This does not mean that man's eyes were continuously fixed on ancient forms or that he felt their influence through a kind of genetic or spiritual transmission (Jung's 'collective unconscious', for example). El Greco had not seen Altamira, but he had studied the Orthodox icons and mosaics.[4] Vivaldi had not heard, either in dreams or through the collective unconscious, the harmonies of pre-gregorian music, but he succeeded in going beyond the musical traditions of his predecessors in Florence. It is modern writers, and only modern writers, who try to 'give a purer meaning to the words of the tribe'.

Another myth or interpretation of art involves the idea that *all art is subservient to reality or to 'nature'*. This belief does not restrict itself to any narrow definitions of 'nature' or 'naturalism', but, in a broader sense, sees art as a possible way of coming to terms with an alien reality and of perceiving it in its true simplicity.

Whether imitating human nature in all its aspects, as European writers and artists (classical, academic, neoclassical and baroque) have tried to do; whether speaking like Chinese painters of the Five Dynasties and in the great plastic themes of the 'way' (*tao*) which allow the artist to immerse himself in the world[5]; whether maintaining the pantheistic role in all dramatic, poetic or musical expression (Goethe, Hölderlin, Nietzsche, Wagner); or whether thinking of literary realism as something which proves either the reality or unreality of the human 'observer' in a world alternately changing and still (Robbe-Grillet) – the principle is never questioned that the work of art is a means of understanding and of coming to terms with the external world.

Certainly, the relationship between artistic creation and exterior reality is constantly affirmed, otherwise one would have to look on art as no more than nostalgic dreaming. And who would question the fact that plastic or imaginary expression requires this kind of relationship with reality? The only guarantee the artist has of success depends on the extent to which he can make a group of people believe in him and respond to his work; he cannot, then, be indifferent to the values of that group. This is precisely what the artist is concerned with: nature as the artist describes it cannot be nature 'as it really is' because it has been twice transformed – once by society and again by the artist. Michel Foucault is right to say, in *Les mots et les choses*, that we only know what the thought-structure of an era allows us to think. On the other hand, the construction of fundamental thought-systems (with which anthropology is well acquainted) in the case of social groups restricted by their environment (i.e. 'archaic' societies) can only be achieved by a necessarily arbitrary classification of the world around them. Such a classification is the measure of approximately how far the group has developed thought-systems and how far social life has become centred round institutions, in the group's adaptation to the environment. In itself this classification is neither absolutely rigid nor absolutely flexible, and it integrates events strictly outside the group's social life – such as death, the destructive effects of a hostile environment, a hurricane or an epidemic – into the recognized art forms of that group. This is the process by which nature, regarded as anti-social and against which the human group pits itself to survive, is brought into society.

This social classification also varies according both to the different groups and types of society involved, and also to the groups and 'classes' within the particular society. It varies to the extent that every image of 'what is natural', of 'nature', of 'reality' reflects the relative norms which constitute normality. Nevertheless, the artist depends on this image of nature as integrated into society.

Now, this image may be used by the artist in such a way that, by the representation of nature, he does in fact glorify man in a form that is particularly meaningful to the social group and set a standard by which to gauge their own energy and dynamism. This is apparent in the work of artists living under centralized monarchies supported by a strong middle class (in seventeenth-century Europe and Japan, for instance), where a 'humanism' based on a particular definition of 'nature' is proudly affirmed. Leaving aside *Discours de la méthode*, a similar combination of reason and nature can be found in that popularizer, Boileau ('perfect reason avoids all extremities'), which was to inspire the builders of palaces, as well as painters and poets of the academic and neo-classical style.

The artist can also struggle against the classifications which a society imposes on him, a society for instance whose systems of values have become more or less hardened and fixed by rigid stratification or by military preoccupations and where there is little opportunity for aspirations of an artistic kind. The artist, *in opposition* to this type of society (and in opposition to the image of nature which it unfolds), affirms 'another' nature. This happened to the Chinese painters at the time of the Yuan dynasty and Mongol invasion,[6] as it did to the German romantics who were imprisoned in the stifling atmosphere of the small principalities exactly at the moment when the French Revolution was opening up hitherto unknown possibilities.

But there again the artist intervenes: what he calls 'nature' is the result of a further transformation which develops and modifies that which society has already made to the universe. Mou-K'i's persimmons and Cézanne's apples are not real fruits, but new classifications at the level of pure meaning. Claude Lévi-Strauss was right when he said to George Charbonnier: 'In so far as the work of art is a sign of the object and not a literal reproduction, it reveals something that was not immediately present in our perception of the object and that is its structure, because the peculiar feature of the language of art is that there exists a profound homology between the structure of the signified and the structure of the signifier.'[7] When artistic creation deals with 'nature', it becomes concerned with something which, in its perception of truth, no longer aims at reality but at the opposite, and this involves a transformation similar to that which society works on the universe. This comparison is not arbitrary, for it involves a *rivalry* as acute as the one which, according to Marcel Mauss, existed between the priest who makes use of the 'manna' of a society to bind that more closely together (*religare*, which in Latin means 'to bind together', has given us the word 'religion') and the sorcerer who uses this same collective force for individual ends. The only reason why the artist effects this transformation is to communicate in new ways, to open up a dialogue and bring about a participation which society cannot create for itself.

No artist, therefore, imitates or merely rediscovers a nature which, already transformed into an image and re-shaped by societies, cultures and different groups, is for him nothing more than a symbol whereby he can increase his audience's participation. What is this 'nature' or 'reality' if not the system of images which a group or a society constructs in order to mirror its mastery over the universe, if not sometimes the triumphant vision of a world completely organized by man's social instincts, and which the artist then transforms strictly according to his own individuality?

In our own time another interpretation of art has often been put forward: *that artistic creation is bound up with*

31

religion and, more generally, with the sacred and, by contrast, with the magical. This theory of art can be found in Nietzsche's writings and in the work of others like Kurt Sachs and Henri Brémond, who have been concerned with art, poetry and dance.[8]

In some types of society it is certainly true that the status given to the artist (or which he gives himself) is similar to that of a priest or a sorcerer. Luc de Heusch has found interesting analogies between the roles of the blacksmith, the artist and the sorcerer in black Africa, analogies which remind us of Prometheus who was the patron of blacksmiths, artists and 'sorcerers' of one sort or another (and punished because they were such) in ancient, rural Greece.[9] However, the analogy ends there because, if their status is comparable, their functions are totally dissimilar: those of the blacksmith or the sorcerer are at the service of the group which chooses them, whereas the artist pursues his own endless search for an elusive role.

This does not prevent the artist from being regarded (not only by the romantics, since Ronsard's *Ode à Michel de l'Hospital* similarly defined the poet's role) as a priest of the absolute, the temporal representative of a sacred power. In fact, this belief takes us back once again to a 'nostalgia for origins', since it refers the confusion of artist and sorcerer to a distant but ever-living past. But more than this, it makes the spectator or the audience participants in a religious rite. By interpreting Antonin Artaud's *The Theatre and its Double* in a certain way, one can reach this same identification of art and the sacred, both being understood as expressions of the terrifying precariousness of life; and this presence of the sacred, since it is not religious, is perfectly compatible with the poet's agnosticism.[10] Neither Jean-Louis Barrault nor Jean Vilar have resisted the temptation to refer, when discussing the theatre, to a 'god-centred' truth.[11] The English pre-Raphaelites and Ruskin, in painting, and romantics like Hugo and Wagner, in poet-

32

ry and music, have all in their own way shared in this ideological sanctification of art.

This theory of art always conceals another one, more appropriate to the position of the 'ecstatic professions' in an industrial society. In such a society – where artistic expression confronts social stratification and a multiplicity of audience and situation, where the old privileged class which previously had the power of fixing values and fashions is in the process of disappearing, and where the artist has an increasingly large public who can make use of the information media to enlarge their range of comparisons (literature, museums, radio, films, television) – what appeared (and we mean *appeared*) to be the characteristic of art in the past is becoming extinct; therefore it is necessary to look for new ways of accounting for the inexplicable. The artist, trapped in the relativism inherent in modern societies, clings to an absolute definition of his role to compensate for the actual weakness of his position. In many cases he acts, often making himself look ridiculous, as a man 'inspired', as though his creative themes were dictated to him by a religious power of which he is the representative on earth. This is not simply a vision of the self-educated or a phantom of resentment, since in one form or another this sacred image of art can be found in Rilke or Stefan Georg, and even at times in Ezra Pound. Need we say that these ideas are completely anachronistic? The artist, whatever his role, is neither the interpreter of some higher force nor does he minister to any cult: creativity is damaged as much by gods as by enthusiasts.

In a well-known passage in *Capital, a Critique of Political Economy*, Marx contrasts ideologies which are beliefs invented by men to explain their position in the world but which do not correspond to reality, to the real knowledge which science, closely linked to actual social experience, can bring. In spite of the difficulties which this distinction[12] creates, it is useful in this context to the extent that the

33

interpretations and definitions of art provided by artists should, in regard to actual creativity, be treated as illusory. If we are trying to grasp the living experience of art, we must take it for what it is: a part of collective experience in which the individual who undertakes it may well justify what he does in one way or another, but in the end must acknowledge it to be an activity in its own right, and not something which can be explained by theories of continuous evolution, primitivism or the sacred.

2 The Application of a Sociology of Art

The sociology of religion has established its own concepts and defined its aims; the sociology of politics has clarified certain principles on which it is based; but the sociology of art lags behind, entangled in the wrong kind of problems.

The most obvious reason for this is that those studying the subject are totally ignorant of the problems associated with artistic creation in all its manifestations, and, more important, are unaware of the kind of experience which artistic creation involves. Neither Charles Lalo, who established the practical and theoretical relations between art and social life,[13] nor Pitirin Sorokin, who suggested an artificial correlation between 'types of culture' and a sense of the absolute, which encloses creative experience in a rigid intellectual framework,[14] fully account for the unique nature of imagined experience.[15]

Not being artists, not even amateurs, it is hardly surprising that they discuss works of art with the incompetence of philistines and remain victims of the prejudices implanted by their teachers. Their understanding of artistic creativity is limited to an academic viewpoint, prisoners as they are of an outdated ideal of 'the beautiful'. In the final analysis, because they are unaware of the changes in outlook taking place around them, they are incapable of properly understanding the enduring creative force of imaginary experience.

As to the sociological part of their work, this is even worse ... Apart from Sorokin who, for reasons which would take too long to examine here, fails to establish any definite correlation between the social dynamism which he postulates and the creativeness of artistic forms, the sociological skill of those who have made attempts in this field has been very restricted. In most cases, they have been concerned to isolate artistic expression to a milieu or else to study the environment of art (the public, the indirect but so-called 'positive' influences), as if this could possibly lead to any serious understanding of the exact nature of artistic creation!

When we refer to the uniqueness of artistic experience, we are not ascribing an autonomous existence to art, with different phases corresponding to the stages of a spiritual activity, raised above and beyond the world, as Heinrich Wölfflin conceived it.[16] However illuminating the theories of this great critic, they are all based on the assumption that artistic creation, especially painting, springs from a purely cognitive activity. He never questions whether the fact that art is deeply rooted in the framework of collective life, far from weakening its force, does not increase its power of communication and even extend its meaning. Benedetto Croce put forward a 'philosophy of art' based on similar principles. He denies that there is the least connection between aesthetics and social life, and he considers that the only plausible study would be an account of the genesis of a work in the artist's mind. According to Croce, when a culture expresses itself through a work of art, the work becomes so uniquely characterized that it cannot be reduced or related to any other level of reality except the absolute which it strives to attain.[17] This is certainly a 'noble' image of artistic creation, the justification of which is doubtless to be found somewhere in the misconceptions of Croce's idealism and in his desire, perhaps understandable in his time, to protect the life of the spirit from any political encroachment.

When we refer to the uniqueness of artistic creation, we are referring to *artistic practice* such as it is enacted in the

36

complex network of human relationships, of groups in conflict or in alliance, and at the level of the many 'dramas' of daily experience where the *wagers* that are authentic works of art are made. If someone were to ask how the authenticity[18] of a work of art was to be established, we would suggest that in this context it depends on two factors: the force of conviction in a work (bearing in mind its explicit aims) and its detachment from financial, ideological and political concerns – in other words, the authentic work of art cannot serve as a justification for any other activity except itself.

This definition should enable us to eliminate from the sociology of art various 'philosophies of art' and even 'aesthetics' whenever these fail to take into account the completely independent nature of artistic creation.[19]

In fact there are only two attempts which at all measure up to the requirements of an authentic sociology of art: that of Georg Lukács, whose ideas were developed more or less faithfully by Walter Benjamin,[20] Theodor Wiesengrand-Adorno and Lucien Goldmann, and that of the Warburg Institute where Erwin Panofsky published the fundamental studies which Pierre Francastel later developed with exceptional richness.[21]

The basic principle of Lukács' thought is undoubtedly, as Georges Gurvitch writes,[22] to find the 'points of attribution' (*Zurechnungspunkt*) of 'works of civilization' to the social structure. This implies that there are two distinct entities which meet (sometimes accidentally) at certain points: that of creative spirituality and that of social life. At the point where Hegelian phenomenology, Dilthey's theories and the Marxist dialectic come together, Lukács thinks it is possible to find some correlation between social experience as a whole and the expression of his own particular age offered by an individual through an imagined representation.

Rejecting any naïve interpretation of Marxism but not what is essential in Marx's thought, Lukács considers that one cannot indiscriminately transfer categories appropriate to capitalist societies to any other social setting (unless such categories are universal), and that it is necessary to find the point of impact or conjunction, *which is different in every instance*, between spiritual possibilities and individual perception of absolute values in society as it is.[23]

That is where the idea of a 'vision of the world' is to be found: by exteriorizing and making concrete the forms of the imagination, a great work of art encounters other formulations which, apparently, differ from it, but which nonetheless have the same logical structure and involve comparable attitudes to, life, death, the 'beyond'. At least, the most important work of art of a particular era acts as a filter for common experience because it embodies, within a *coherent* system and style, the *possible* problems which contemporaries may encounter and sometimes resolve in practical life.

Because it connects together different works of art, the idea of a 'vision of the world' becomes a *model* of life and existence by uniting disparate artistic expressions in a common inspiration. In contrast to popular materialism, which superimposes arbitrary concepts on an already dogmatic and rigid interpretation of reality, this idea enables us to place a work of art in its existential, everyday human perspective. Similarly, one can juxtapose different 'visions of the world', thereby including a number of artists within the framework of a single era.

In *The Hidden God* and also *Racine*, Lucien Goldmann has given a striking account of the way in which literary history can represent a period dramatically. He contrasts the casuistical and official 'vision of the world' held in the *grand siècle* to that of the French Jansenists, who renounced the 'king's service' and rejected all compromise with the world in order to seek in solitude a human experience 'under the eye of God'. Goldmann takes this conflict of spiritual values in the seventeenth century and applies it to literature by bringing together the apparently dissimilar attitudes of Barcos, Pascal and Racine, and comparing them to the prevailing attitude of compromise with the social and political world which demanded a practical morality, to quieten man's problems concerning God and to divert him from a preoccupation with the absolute.

One can understand the fascination of such approaches. They enable us to see the characteristics of a particular period under a new arrangement, and to recapture dramatic features of the period which traditional criticism has neglected. They even enable us to describe a Marxist vision of the world, as Goldmann attempted to do in *Récherches dialectiques*[24] – though, it is true, his attempt is extremely intellectualized and in reality does not find expression in any work of art, except partially in Malraux or in Brecht where it appears in a fervently ideological form.

The importance of this theory for a sociology of art is more debatable. There are several objections to it, both from the point of view of the theory and of the practice of art:

1. Although the internal cohesion of a work of art might seem necessary to justify the association of imagined forms with general models and to make a connection between the style of a work of art and a 'vision of the world', in fact, it is a very problematical issue. The cohesion in a work of art or in a style is no more than the result of the particular characteristics of a temperament or of a personality; it would be absurd to try to establish that Hölderlin or Rimbaud or any musician or painter was preoccupied with this.

Besides, the apparent superiority given by Lukács and Goldmann to literature constitutes a real danger for any interpretation: it is an entirely intellectual assumption to place such a high regard on the written word, since this coherence is hardly only found in literature.

2. It is equally debatable whether an individual can deal with an entire era: to think that a great artist crystallizes in himself the widespread problem of his time and that he embodies in his work an entire civilization is to accept a romantic image which does not correspond to reality. Surely one should realize that the artist and artistic understanding transcend social structures, environments and the petty struggles of groups or factions which always impinge upon a writer or a creative artist?

In addition, this interpretation neglects or ignores the many aspects of real life that cannot be perceived by a single individual, whatever his social status. The fact, too, that it concerns a model valid for a few individuals, remarkable for their talent, means that this model corresponds, or should correspond, to a 'normality', that is to say, to human attitudes which are universal. However, in art we might well ask if these general models do define the importance of a work of art.

Thus, when Lukács studies Goethe he makes the German writer into the representative of everything his era contained, all the possibilities of experience belonging to his period in history. But Lukács' interpretation surely fails to take into account Goethe's situation, because although Goethe was in contact with the leading intellectuals of his time, he was nevertheless restricted by his ministerial work in the Weimar. Also, Lukács ignores the fact that the writings of Lenz, Büchner, Kleist and Hölderlin (whom Goethe kept at a distance and rather despised) could open up perspectives which cannot be found in Goethe. Because these artists did not, like Goethe, achieve social (nor apparently artistic) success, must we therefore treat them as insignificant or try somehow to fit them into Goethe's thought, which in any case they rejected? To look upon Goethe as the model of what is 'normal' and acceptable in human life would be simply to confuse prejudice with judgement, and would be to allow preference (for the superiority of a particular type of expression) to enter into an apparently objective analysis.*

Is not this interpretation influenced by the alarming theory which Hegel propounded when he was an old man: the identification of objectivity with success, of reason with social or political domination? In *The Historical Novel* Lukács falls into this trap. He compares Shakespeare with other Elizabethan dramatists on the grounds that *Romeo and Juliet* represents 'normal love', while the other playwrights base their work on incest and adultery! As if *Hamlet* or *Richard II* were models of 'normality' and represented the kind of experiences which contemporaries of these plays had or might have been through.

3. Finally, Lukács and his disciples regard the work of art as having, in its own right, an awareness of the world and of 'man' (in the nineteenth-century humanist sense). That they should do so is not surprising in view of the fact that they have formulated a theory in which the artist is regarded as receiving, momentarily, problems which existed before him, and which have been already posed either by events or by the questioning of a previous era. The whole process assumes that the work of art interprets and reconstructs, in an imagined whole, themes which had emerged in the past.[25]

But this is to ignore two things. First, that the framework of human relationships – whether they be multiple, contradictory, harmonious or parallel – comprises much more than the artist's experience of the world. The artist's particular experience is only one of the many possible kinds of human experience, and in no way can it be seen as the embodiment of a 'milieu'. Within this complex but living (and often

* From the same point of view, it would be only too easy to set up the official Soviet novelist of the Stalinist era as the only valid model of artistic endeavour – to the exclusion of the non-conformist 'rebel' poets and artists who were nevertheless the only ones whose names have survived. This theory of the political conqueror is condemned by all Marxist philosophy.

confused) framework, the artist tries to make himself understood by rejecting all *a priori* definitions of what the world or God ought to be (and often condemning the ideologies in which he has been brought up). If he does not try to make himself understood in this way, which borders on the unattainable (and which only exists in so far as it succeeds in provoking a response), the artist will be nothing but a 'craftsman' or an 'academic'.

Second, the idea that the artist reflects and crystallizes the basic characteristics of his time leads to 'academicism'. This deliberately neglects the prophetic power of artistic creation, and ignores the capacity of the imagination to anticipate the actual experience of men in a certain period. For example, it was only after a slow, prolonged and laborious study by art of space that people began to speak about 'perspective'; nineteenth-century novels and poetry have profoundly influenced middle and upper-class mentality; the idea of space which the Cubist painters, the Surrealists and Dadaists worked on for a long time, has now become an integral part of our daily lives, from advertisements in the underground to covers of magazines and even 'Pop Art'.

In reality, every artistic experience of the creation of forms is – to use an image from card-playing – a 'new deal' which, while undoubtedly making use of essential elements from the 'human landscape' inhabited by the artist (whether this landscape is in his mind or actual), suggests a new arrangement and a redistribution of the established system. Art is very rarely the representation of an order. Rather, it continuously and anxiously opposes and questions it. Even Goethe is no exception to this rule. If he was, would we still continue to read him today?

For all these reasons, the attempt of Lukács and his disciples would appear to have failed: they have not been able to place the work of art in the living perspective of art today nor in relation to what amateurs or today's public read and re-read, admire or listen to. Every time they try to explain modern creativity, what results are the inadequacies or banalities of the kind which occur when Lukács writes about Joyce or Beckett. In fact, it is not art they are concerned with, but the translation of philosophical problems into visual images. This has nothing to do with real experience.

The real importance of the Warburg School, on the other hand, is to have made the problem of the relationship between art and collective life central to any study of creative activity. For it is in this relationship that a more or less successful inter-action takes place, between the intellectual speculative process applied to social experience, the full sense of personal creativity at the moment of aesthetic invention, and the conscious acknowledgement of the potential of this creativity to communicate and suggest meanings, capable of uniting the collective experience of different groups, and even of society as a whole. Certainly, this general description includes some elements which belong to Panofsky and others which come from Francastel, himself influenced by the thought of Marcel Mauss. But their approach is similar, in that it is based on what both might have called an 'archaeology' of the fundamental structures of imaginative experience.

When he discusses space, Erwin Panofsky puts the problem of plastic art in its true perspective, by rescuing it from a rigidly dogmatic definition of space as three-dimensional and governed by the laws of perspective. He reminds us appropriately that what *we* call 'space' is not a 'constant' in the whole of human experience, but is something which has gradually evolved, with effects that are felt in many aspects of daily life in Europe.

It is Pierre Francastel who has developed these ideas in an original way. Taking Panofsky's analysis which describes the transition from '*espace-agrégat*' to '*espace-système*', based on a combination of art and mathematics, Francastel reverses the conventional data. The space which he studies is artificial; it might just as well not have existed and is arbitrary just as our portrayal of man is not itself the only rational or possible one.

It is not, as we might believe, from a greater accuracy in perception or from a greater realism or accuracy in analysing reality that this transformation comes, since what we call reality only exists as the mental structure which we develop in order to create an image of it. The painter constructs and fabricates the nature of reality. He even builds up the image of the town in which he lives – the Florence which the architects built first came to life in the Florence which the artists painted in their pictures. The thought of the period we call the 'Renaissance' began with an evaluation of the actual relationships between objects and things, and ended with the representation of cubic space in which the vanishing lines of perspective converge at a single point in the background of the painting – a discovery which forced the artist to find a relationship between tonal and linear design. To make symbolic what experience has suggested as factual was an immense undertaking. And it should not be confused with subsequent intellectualizations made by painters who, without advancing any new spatial theory, take over what has been achieved before them and which, with time, has become an unchallenged fact. We have to wait for the nineteenth century for new spatial and artistic theories. This time the symbols of the *Trecento*, which had become unquestioned facts, were treated by the painter and the intellectual as only hypothetical.[26]

Francastel sets out to establish a sociology of art through the examination of a work of art in the early stages of its creation, as if he was investigating the basic elements which constitute our experience of life and society. Through this approach he has given the sociology of art one of its most important methodological concepts. He concentrates on that point where the work of art is not yet dead and consigned to a museum, but is in its moment of creative

44

vitality. Francastel does not give factual descriptions a value in themselves, thereby avoiding the false problem of realism, nor does he reduce creativity to one of the mythologies which falsify it. Instead, he sees creative expression as a collective and individual activity influencing human experience itself and giving us an opportunity to reach a definition of ourselves in a world which we gradually come to dominate.

In this sense, his analysis is one of the most important contributions to a 'Marxist' approach to the sociology of art, if this term has any meaning. In one of the most searching studies of the existential and philosophical development of Marx, Henri Lefebvre, commenting on *Economic and Philosophical Manuscripts of 1844*, wrote: 'The eye becomes human when its object becomes the social and human object, originating in man and directed towards man. The senses thus "directly and as calculated by theoreticians" become transformed and impregnated by social life, by "reason" – having power over the object.'[27] If we accept that this gets to the heart of Marxism (in so far as exteriorization and alienation are not confused, as they are in Hegel), then Francastel's studies extend this train of thought and give it meaning. Space becomes a problem because through it man gains a social solidarity which is independent of that mystical intuition of reality which materialists claim exists. The origin and growth of creative activity are the same as those of social life, and social life rediscovers in the creative individual the principles and driving force through which it is transformed.

Even without detailed analysis, it is not difficult to see that Francastel's attempt is limited to the study of mental structures. It is true that he discusses relativity, but only in reference to the part it played in debates on the nature of space in the fourteenth and nineteenth centuries. He does not make relativity central to his argument, and only examines one particular aspect of space, in which the sociological analysis discovers a number of different social experiences of space.[28] This plurality does not weaken his argument but it does limit its application, because in other areas of creativity, even in the period Francastel discusses, we can find various experiences of space which frequently differ from the one he chooses to adopt. In the period which Francastel studies, for example, only the enclosed stage, which later became the Italian theatre (the magic or baroque theatre) corresponds to the theories expressed in painting. The dramatic innovations of the Elizabethans or of the Spanish, the fairground theatre and the more or less spontaneous forms of drama – none of these depend on these factors but rather on other experiences of space taken from life.[29] And one could also mention baroque representations which were themselves so diverse that the experience of 'space' presented by the baroque of Latin America and Central Europe appears radically different.

This relativity in the experience of space means that we should not give exclusive importance to the representation of space in painting. And this should also remind us that space is more than just one element in experience, because as soon as it is regarded as a symbol (something Francastel ably demonstrates) it becomes a projection of real experience, an exploration of the mind which goes beyond actual emotions. This is not only because the representations of painters or artists can become real, but also because the experimental vision becomes the matrix of hitherto unknown emotions.

On the other hand, if we admit that space, as conceived and practised by artists, implies an added appropriation of the human and social substance by a particular age in history, the 'point of attribution' of such an appropriation must be placed in its precise social context. We must see this in the context of a continuous demand made by the whole of society, springing from the aggressive co-existence of groups and communities within the framework of collective life. When we find that a work of art possesses social substance or 'manna', we have to analyse intellectually the forms which represent it, even if they are imagined ones.

Finally, another danger which threatens this approach to a sociology of art is that there is a risk of bringing back the old and sterile distinction between form and content. By concentrating on the formative stages of structures and on the elements which compose experience, Panofsky and Francastel – undoubtedly influenced by Kant's presuppositions – only examine one moment in the creative process, leaving aside the element of communication and overt meaning which, if one wants to describe the latter in terms of real collective experience, is necessarily implied. It can be misleading to define the sociology of artistic creation only by its 'archaeological' and not by its effective characteristics. The meaning of a work of art not only lies in its origin but also in its purpose, what it wants to achieve and the extent to which it influences the perception of others.

However, Francastel was aware of this limitation and surmounted the problem of an over-narrow structural genealogy by evolving his theory of the 'representative object, the object of civilization'.[30] Being strongly opposed to the restriction of the sociology of art to linguistics or mathematics, he considers that one will create 'a sociology of art only by trying to understand the artistic experience of the present day'. It is in this light that we should formulate working hypotheses which will enable us *to understand the totality of the artistic experience within the totality of social experience.**

---

* We should also mention here another attempt to explain the work of art which is based on a particular terminology which analyses the work through its forms of expression. But this is to overlook what Maurice Merleau-Ponty reminded us of a few days before his death – that language is less in harmony with the unconscious and all its levels than it is with the actual perception of reality (in *L'Inconscient*, Conference of Benneval, ed. by Dr Ely, Desclée de Brouver). These attempts at analysis which proceed by using a motley of terms borrowed from the

The application of a sociology of art consists, therefore, of specifying certain working hypotheses which are neither intellectual presuppositions nor dogmatic definitions but tools for analysis, without any prior definitions of terms or contents. Instead of 'dividing up' artistic creation into pieces which can never recombine into a living unity, we must find a method of analysis which neither falsifies sociology nor distorts the work of art.

One of the mistakes which has diverted the sociology of art from its true path has been the dissection of a work's genesis through the application of such specious contrasts as 'subjective' and 'objective', the 'inner' and the 'outer' and so on. Therefore, the first working hypothesis we shall put forward will be that of *drama*.

We use this word with the same meaning as George Politzer in his *Fondements de la psychologie*.[31] 'Drama' implies a concrete situation – using the adjective here to balance the emotive associations of the word 'situation'. On the other hand, 'drama' means the splitting up of individual experience in so far as this is composed of a conflict, a planned action, an intrigue, in which the majority of 'actors' who define its place within collective life participate.

'Drama' involves the behaviour of individuals gathered into a changing whole, a process which allows an actual dramatization during which we play a role, struggle against an obstacle, give up, sometimes win, sometimes lose. It is within this framework that, as Politzer rightly says, human

---

dictionaries of rhetoric, *translate* the work of art into *meta-language*, that is to say, with less regard for the living reality experienced and in fact controlled by the creative artist than for the changing forms of expression. In this way, these forms become distorted and shorn of their true significance. From a sociological point of view this is typical of the unfortunate state of mind of non-creative intellectuals who look to criticism (original or otherwise) as a consolation for their own inadequacy. In most cases, it bears a resemblance to what Nietzsche called 'the judgement formed by resentment'. It also helps us to understand the low value put on the imagination in Western countries today.

meanings become valid. But drama is not only a *praktische Menschenkenntnis*, since the process by which a planned action is described also holds a meaning which goes beyond (at least for the observer) what the dramatic character expects of his actions or his feelings. Therefore, one can claim 'that in the dramatic experience there is a perception increased by understanding' which, through analysis and the staging of drama and its vital components, 'relates everything to experience'.

In a sociology of art, we define *drama* as a combination of behaviour, emotions, attitudes, ideologies, actions and creations which, *for the creative individual*, crystallizes the whole of society and places the genesis of a work of art within the complex of those contradictory forms which make up collective life. Thus drama as defined by Shakespeare's works must take into account the poet's position in a society which was affected by real, if hardly perceptible, changes – the power-orientated ideologies of the bourgeoisie, the latin and Italianizing education of the artist, as well as his personal singularity as an artist, the relationship between psychological themes (which psychoanalysis can detect if it re-integrates them into the working of the whole) and the existing literary forms. In short, all that explains why Shakespeare turned to drama and what he hoped to achieve by the figuration and symbolic exaltation of certain recurrent or representative themes.

At least this prevents us from reducing the work of art to mere biography or vice-versa, since we are trying to understand the latent meaning of the themes in the light of the success or otherwise of the attempt to exteriorize and objectify them. And the true significance of this attempt depends on the importance of what is concealed. Just as Shakespearian themes cannot simply be understood as collective representations of his time, so they cannot be reduced to personal, psychological manifestations. In order to decipher them, we must integrate them into the system of dramatic signs which the poet depicts and whose meaning, beyond their circumstantial origin, we have to grasp.

A further advantage of this hypothesis is that it enables us to place the work of art within a living whole which momentarily is embodied in the artist. This means that we do not have to make any distinction between subjective and objective 'points of view', since we can regard its different practical aspects as the divergent directions in which mental and social experiences proceed from the real situation, and as the necessary involvement both of an artist's personality in his own work and of the work of art in a society where the artist must assert himself.

It equally prevents us from separating form and content, that division which is merely arbitrary and secondary, created by theorists who are unaware that creative experience is heterogeneous and universal. By using the word 'drama' we can understand *form* as a particular attempt of the imagination to discover the common origin of certain elements to which everyone can respond emotionally (the 'genetic structures' of Francastel), and *content* as the imaginary attempt to create immediate meanings which require a spontaneous mental response from an audience.

Finally, this hypothesis lends justification to the kind of critical study which speaks about a work of art as an attempt to overcome an obstacle – of the inadequate power of others to receive an unexpected or barely comprehensible message, of the alienation and dispersal or rigid separation of people into castes, classes and groups, and of changes in the meaning of images. In other words, this obstacle consists of everything that prevents the total communication which the artist, whatever his materials, cannot choose but try to realize.*

* The distinction which Alain was fond of making between the various materials available to the artist (stone, the written word, colour and so on) adds nothing to our present analysis except a description, admittedly often useful, of a particular craft.

Something of this concept can be found in the second working hypothesis which we propose, that of *the polemic sign*. And one of the reasons which leads us to define the sign as a 'group of activities', a demonstration of psycho-social behaviour, is in order to oppose the extreme poverty of its present-day meaning. For nowadays, it has only an abstract connotation, gesturing towards a coherent theory which arranges disparate elements into a system which may be challenged as being subjective despite its pretensions to the contrary.

Now, if we look at the proper meaning of the sign, then we see that it has a double function (and is not just one thing or a simple activity): the assumption that there is an obstacle (either of participation or expression) to be overcome, and the real or imagined attempt to overcome the obstacle.[32] This striving towards effective communication, this technical attempt to communicate through a particular element which indicates but does not constitute the whole, means that the work of art becomes a more or less coherent system of actions, whether suggested or explicit, directed at real communication. This is what endows the work of art with a dynamic value of which perhaps even the artist himself is unaware.

Such a *polemic* definition also enables us to define the real impediment with which the artist's imagination grapples. Sometimes it can take the form of suffering or a physiological illness, either overcome or sublimated (El Greco's optical defect, the deafness of Goya and Beethoven, Nietzsche's nervous disease and so on), but this is never the complete explanation, because the physical barrier is often only the symbol of another, that of a temporary blockage in the free inter-communication of human sensibility. In addition, this impediment can be of the kind that is erected, very consciously though in a disguised form, by social classes to block the ambition of men like Jean Racine who, as Raymond Picard has pointed out,[33] used poetry as a means of social advancement. Or the obstacle can be of the kind erected by stratified societies to block the opportunity for individual advancement, which in fact has been explicitly offered to all men by historical and political changes (such as was the position of the intellectual after the French Revolution when 'Caesar-like' heroes, broken by society, were created, such as Julien Sorel, Frédéric Moreau or Rubempré). Not only this, it can be the supreme obstacle, as adapted and sublimated by metaphysics, of total non-communication, and of the absurd and the solitary (Hölderlin, Kafka).

Whatever the factual character of such an impediment, it does at least enable us to understand that every significant imagined action is *a communication from a distance which is never reconciled to this distance*. We say 'from a distance' because if men did not have to reach out to *one another*, separated by space and time, through the barriers created by groups and classes, they would not need to rely on signs any more than on the imaginary. Instead men would equally participate in the social substance. But we cannot hope to achieve this, any more than Kant's dove could hope to fly beyond the field of gravity where its wings would be powerless and it would drift forever.

The advantage of such a working hypothesis is obvious. It integrates the imaginary, in all its creative forms, into human life and gives to what traditional psychology – and all too often sociology – calls a 'function' the reality of a course of action, of purposeful activity. If we understand the shaping imagination as an activity involved in existence and continuously threatened, then the work of art takes on a new dimension. And it becomes no longer possible, fortunately, to break it down into abstractions.

Another working hypothesis which a well-founded sociology of art ought to use, is that of *the conjunction of the natural and the social systems of classification.* However, these systems do require a sociological explanation.

In a well-known passage in *The Elementary Forms of the Religious Life*, Durkheim discusses the *genera*, the ideas of genus and class which are the first elements of conceptual thought, or, at least, the raw material which individual conceptual thought will employ later. He thinks it is possible to prove that these first structures of nomenclature correspond to the forms of social organization, in other words, to the arrangement of groups and individuals in the same community. 'It is because men had established groups' he says 'that they were able to group things', and this explains why the first mental systems were similar to the systems of social organization, and why linguistic interchange was modelled on the exchange of services, goods or women.[34]

If we think 'it is society which has supplied the basis for logical thought', then the ordinances which govern the classifications are the result of a double effort: to integrate the natural world into society, and to understand the natural world in terms of the social categories which have been formed.

In this double activity which binds closely together mental and social classifications, we can recognize one of the fundamental elements of man's collective and individual experience.[35] Ignoring the fact that Durkheim gave 'the totemic phenomenon' an importance which modern ethnology disputes – since he considers that the 'content' of these classifications depends primarily, in its most primitive and basic form, on the elements clarified by the acceptance of a single emblem[36] – one is nevertheless confronted by a highly important analysis, some aspects of which Marcel Mauss has mentioned in *Essai sur le don*. Surely this analysis helps us to see that the endeavour to make classifications is an affirmation of the fact that society is dynamic, since such classifications are an attempt on the part of society to structure the natural world.

Human groups are persistent in their attempt, which in the beginning is almost hallucinatory, to transform into classified terms, and then into signs and symbols, certain natural forces which in themselves cannot be grasped except through the effects (always negative) which they have on the community. From the moment we judge the life of these communities according to the extent they are subjected to external forces (ecological, geographical or climatic), each of these representations (which can become crystallized into myths) will appear to spring from a society's attempt (successful or otherwise) to oppose 'nature'. But this is still a primitive kind of Prometheanism in which individual consciousness is glorified.

Bearing this in mind, we can see how these classifications represent the degree of vitality present in societies, especially in the case of societies which exteriorize, by rites or mimes and dances a way of life which has been laboriously achieved in the face of the natural aggressiveness of 'nature'. When taken in isolation and detached from the existential framework which supports them, these classifications can suggest, through their encounter with the system of social classifications, other symbols which the solidarity of the group does not immediately use.

In the majority of cases, however, the encounter between natural and social elements, within the framework of a single structure of classification, creates a new system which corresponds to what *we* call 'art' in 'primitive' and also in certain advanced societies. Certainly, this is not an invariable law and it would be impossible to prove that such encounters occur in all types of society. But at least one can say that when this encounter occurs with a certain intensity, imaginative symbolism appears which is expressed through diverse activities, depending on the various materials available – masques, dances, bush-drum music, as well as cave paintings and straight-forward painting or music.

It is as though the artistic sign appears whenever there is an encounter between the signs of classification which integrate the natural world into society and the signs which designate social activity itself, and, at that meeting point, between the systems which organize the dissolvant natural forces and the systems which regulate human relationships. Such an encounter overcomes both the system whose function is only that of integration and also the temporary framework which contains this. And the artistic sign is 'a group of meanings', all the more unsettling because it is always created by an atypical individual, someone who frees himself from immediate reality by putting forward an order and a new arrangement which offers a different image of man from the one exteriorized by rites and official collective representations.

One can see how such an hypothesis can justify interpretations of art based on the 'return to the origins' or to the 'sources', or on the myth of the 'primitive', because in primitive societies, just as in our own, artistic signs can correspond to the encounter within a simple structure between classifications depending on 'nature' and those depending on society. It is a homogeneity which brings them close together, and not a continuity inherent in the progression of history, whose irreversibility art is magically supposed to be able to rise above.

These structures of meanings which bring together different kinds of classification can be found at different levels of artistic creation. What is the point of arguing about whether Siou Tao-ning, a Chinese painter of the Sung dynasty, faithfully represented nature by painting on long scrolls a sequence of mountain ranges, clouds and lakes, inhabited by minuscule people? He managed to combine in an original way two types of classification which, when they are brought together, make a world of shifting perspective, an immense landscape for the spectator's dreams. In Japan, the traditions of *Ikebana*, the art of flower arrangement, illustrate the remarkable success of similar encounters between different structures. As Tadao Yama-moto[37] said: 'the flower is there not only to be admired, but to be identified with human life'. This identification is based on encounters between two different kinds of well-ordered signs. And in front of this abstract combination, one has adequate opportunity to indulge in dreaming.

An African mask is also the result of a comparable synthesis of divergent signs. A 'painted mask' of Mali, for example, combines the form of the human face with natural or merely strange images – an old shoddy mirror hung on the left cheek, cowries, a rusty key. It is as if the image of man has to come from the encounter between these divergent classifications, as if the mask captures briefly a fusion of elements taken from different realms.

But these types of encounter are not unique to the art of the East or of 'archaic' societies. One of the reasons why critics have spoken so inadequately about non-representational painting from Klee onwards is that their language, which was adapted to impressionist or even cubist art, has been unable to find words to describe the inter-action of signs in their simplest form, and instead of analysis they have gone on indulging in metaphysical fantasies. But, in fact, non-representational painting has been an attempt (at least by the best artists) to re-unite classifications which are already in a symbolic form and which belong to different systems. This is highly characteristic of Klee, especially at the time of his two journeys to the East. Not only did he discover that forms and colours were broken up by the intensity of sun and light, but he also made use of ideogrammes which are similar to the systems of social classification used by the Bedouins of the Tunisian desert. What he works out from these encounters, he integrates into his world of colours. It is not the historical origin of these classifications which is so important, but the fact that they combine together in the mind of a great artist.[38]

In other figurative painters, the encounter between these two orders also achieves great intensity. For example, by borrowing elements of a classification from movement and dance forms which combine other signs drawn from Kabyle–Berber symbolism, Atlan created an original language whose force lies in the fragile complexity of such a combination.[39]

In music, the recent studies of Pierre Schaffer have a similar tendency. In this context Xenakis' musical piece *Terrêtektorh** is highly illuminating, especially as he is a musician who has always made use of signs belonging to his own native traditional expression. The positioning of the audience amongst the orchestra produces a visual musical performance which no stereophonic arrangement could equal. And the combination of atonic sounds, from siren whistles, maraccas, whips and wood-blocks, suggests a musical space in which natural sounds (falling hailstones, cicada stridulation, anything at all) are arranged. Undoubtedly, among modern musicians, it is Boulez and Nono who exploit to the full these mixed structures of classifications of different and apparently incompatible origins.

In choreography one finds these mixed structures especially in Maurice Béjart's work, where the artist combines, as in *Érotica*, *Vénusberg* or *Le boléro*, certain elements taken from erotic human signs which he then interweaves with the movements taken from 'primitive' dance and with hieroglyphic signs designating pure gestures. This allows him to counteract through choreography the outdated significance of a piece of music – as he did with the *Adagio* of Beethoven's *Ninth Symphony*. The *pas de deux* which he composed is a powerful criticism of Beethoven's religious sentimentalism.†

Finally, the last two working hypotheses we suggest as the basis for a sociology of the imaginary are those of *anomy* and the *atypic*. These complement each other but still remain distinct in their points of application. And it should be said at once that they ought to make it possible for sociology to

* Composed for the Festival of Royan in 1965.
† Danced by Tania Bari and Jorge Lefèvre.

explain individual productions independently from the tradition of an outdated positivism.

The concept of anomy enables us to retain a link with classical sociology and to give a new meaning to one of the most useful terms suggested by Durkheim, in his definition of what has become modern sociology. According to Durkheim, every society creates a precarious but positive balance between groups, tendencies, mentalities and particular demands, by managing to satisfy certain needs. This occurs when military glory, religion or magic are adequate to satisfy all human needs. In this situation, the system by which society is regulated and the flexibility of groupings encourage mild internal changes, and are sufficient to control any forces or, at least, to channel them into integration.

When structures are stable like this, man does not try to overthrow the barriers which the group has imposed on him and in which he has been brought up. He only desires what his position in the group allows him to desire, whatever corresponds to the models or to the system of established values. His sources of satisfaction are strictly allocated by the ideal which everyone implicitly accepts, and there is a hierarchy of desires just as there is a hierarchy of social status and classes. 'Under this pressure, each in his own sphere vaguely realizes the limits his ambition can reach and does not aspire to anything beyond them.'[40]

However, when these structures are modified, either because of war or peaceful inter-action with another group, or because the internal dynamism of the society, acting upon its own established forms, overthrows them without having first instituted another social order to replace them, then people become agitated and the balance is disrupted. The established ideal loses its prestige and the 'scale of values which previously regulated needs no longer remains the same'. This leads to a state of *disorder* which causes an upsurge of demands and desires.

The concept of anomy derives from this, for it refers to the overall state of disorder caused by the continuous process of change in the social structure. Whether such changes are sudden or gradual, whether they are spread over two or three centuries or occur in a few decades, the important factor is that people, separated from the norms which until then controlled and ordered their desires, suddenly find themselves confronted with unrestricted aspirations.

At this point, however, we disagree with Durkheim whose obdurate moralism leads him to prefer a 'social harmony' which is another way of saying 'moral order'. This 'erethism', which he regards as a cause of suffering and distress, appears to us, on the contrary, to be an important factor in the creation of new human possibilities. During these periods of disorder or anomy, both collective and individual freedom find expression in small or nation-wide 'dramas', and can even produce hitherto unknown opportunities, capable of creating stable relationships and real development.

In the course of this transition from one social structure to another, the mental or spiritual life of men becomes more intense because it does not exhaust itself trying to live up to certain models. Man sees himself 'condemned to freedom' and thrown beyond himself into a new image, which can take a negative form and which is far from being a symbol of integration capable of realization at some later date. And so this individual or collective spiritual life, which can no longer be expressed or fulfilled within the structures of an already disintegrating society, moves towards the imaginary and the creation of new forms.

It would certainly be absurd to regard the transformation of the social structure and the disorder this produces as the only cause and condition of artistic creation. Nonetheless, it should be pointed out that the great creative periods nearly all coincide with such upheavals. The Greek theatre was at its height when the effects of the slow transition from patriarchal rural life, impregnated with feudal traditions, to urban life was being felt with greatest intensity.* European drama was at its peak at the moment when the world of the Middle Ages, after two centuries, was moving into the pre-modern world of centralizing and state-controlled monarchies, as in Spain or in England. The modern painter of the Paris School lived at a time when liberal or commercial societies were giving way to modern industrial societies.

The particular importance of the concept of anomy lies in the fact that it enables us to take into account the phenomena of individual and collective creativity which otherwise might appear simply as aberrations or incapable of classification. The fact that, for example, all the early Greek or Elizabethan dramas were based on crime and murder is not the mark of a lawless and barbaric era; it is the sign or the symbol of an anxiety caused by the impossibility of continuing to live according to traditional norms. And the response which these *represented* crimes provoke is much greater because it also implies the desire for a new human order, in accordance with a dialectic one often finds in history.†

Every system of facts (not only in the realm of artistic creation) becomes clearer when one applies to it the concept of anomy. It throws a new light on the facts by enabling us to make an analysis which does not reduce them to a vague collective summary.

In contrast, the significance of the concept of the atypic is more limited, but it acquires its full meaning in those

---

* If Greece had remained a rural society, she would never have victoriously withstood the Persians. The transition, though implicit and hesitant, contributed to that tension which resulted in the victory at Salamis, the consequences of which were directly registered in the drama.

† This is the limitation of Artaud's observations in *The Theatre and its Double*. He discusses, in very general terms, pure violence, while surely such violence symbolizes a questioning of human order and the re-establishment of that order.

societies which only have one system of values, where the homogeneity of society is complete – whether in archaic societies or in a society where social homogeneity is sufficiently complete, as in the modern technological culture of the United States. And undoubtedly it is not by chance that American anthropologists have put forward this concept in order to analyse 'primitive' facts.

As we understand this concept, it is necessary to find the point of attribution of 'artistic' forms to individual life. Without this encounter it would be impossible to transform common representations through personal and arbitrary intervention (what one calls 'style'). This 'point of attribution' is a determining factor in that it enables us to grasp the true perspectives of certain activities which historians and philosophers are liable to reduce to simple formulas.

The scientific meaning which Margaret Mead has given to the atypic is all the more emphatic because she regards culture as a specific and completely indispensable reality, to the detriment of society itself. In *Sex and Temperament in Three Primitive Societies* she refers to the human ideal created by the Arapesh and the individuals who withdrew into solitude, which, if these individuals lived among the Mundugamor, would be seen as a form of active participation. What is exceptional or deviant in one group becomes normal in another – and vice-versa. This even suggests that the problem of deviation could be simply solved by a change of location.

But Margaret Mead does not seem to understand the significance of the terms she uses. She refers to certain deviations which she calls 'atypical' without realizing that the atypic cannot be restricted to a definition which is exclusively negative or partial. Her rather facile terminology fails to take into account the positive influence a deviation exerts when it is expressed consciously. Although she points out that in most of the groups she has studied individualism results from a socio-cultural selection based on physiological characteristics (the cripple from birth or the albino has, statistically speaking, more chance of being selected than other people), she does not seem to understand nor to be able to evaluate the consequences of this discovery. In fact, the designation by society of an individual as someone who necessarily has to be separated from others, or the realization (often sad and painful) by a member of a group that it is impossible for him to integrate himself into the accepted stereotypes (i.e. into the cultural ideal which forms the basis of personality), places on this particular individual the social essence of the group, its 'manna'. This essence can either destroy him or else he can use it for his own advantage in the search for new forms of participation.

Finally, Margaret Mead does not fully realize that a culture can be made up of as many possible and probable elements as actual ones. In her well-known chapter on the 'atypical individual', she fails to understand that various forms of heresy can be anything other than variants or inversions of the dichotomy between the sexes, a dichotomy she tends to emphasize so strongly that the two become completely separate entities.

Nevertheless, she does state clearly that the atypical individual requires and sometimes finds in painting, in mask making, in music or dancing, the means of expressing his feeling of isolation. But this 'feeling of isolation' is nothing but an indication of a real need to participate which the individual, in spite of himself, inwardly feels.

If we use this concept without restricting it to a straight dichotomy between normal and abnormal, we should be able to see in the works produced by these atypical individuals (masks, tapa, bush-drum music and so on) the diverse representations created by individuals responsible for imagined expression as well as the outline of possible relationships and of likely forms of participation.

Art in this context does not belong to the level of collective life where we find common ideas or a 'collective unconscious'. Rather, it involves the questioning of human relationships by an individual whose isolation has made him likely to evolve new forms of relationship and alternative social groupings.

However limited the meaning of the concept of the atypic in comparison to that of anomy, it does enable us to understand the creation of imagined signs in those societies where art does not have importance, or where the representation of elements which are not real springs from a violent need for full participation which sometimes makes use of religion, sometimes of magic and sometimes of politics, to express itself. Therefore, it is a misconception to link the arts with the sacred or with magic, since these are nascent forms which, through the most important areas of collective experience, are trying to discover ways of participation which are denied by everything else.

Drama, the polemic sign, the structures of different classifications, anomy and the atypic, are only working hypotheses. They serve as a basis for analysis and enable us to pick out from the whole of experience certain significant underlying facts which can then be interpreted. It goes without saying that these terms are only valid in relation to a living society which is the background to everything that is represented. And this background is also the dynamic principle and driving force, because each of its aspects only has meaning in the continuous movement of change which makes society what it is. To understand the meaning of artistic creation, we have to work out a coherent picture of social creation.

3   Art in Society, Society in Art

The 'working hypotheses' we have just outlined do not in themselves throw much light on the experience of artistic creation. They are deficient in what 'aesthetics' or 'philosophies of art' also lack: a sociological viewpoint or even an awareness of modern sociological thinking.

Artistic creation in all its various forms can never be reduced to our present-day understanding of it nor to certain of its elements which are arbitrarily chosen from periods in the past. To be more precise, we cannot separate the imagination from the general influences active at the time when the work of art was created, because it is impossible to detach the imagination from social reality. We can only establish the extent to which a particular artistic expression is rooted in society by analysing all the social symbols which are crystallized in it and which it in turn crystallizes in its development.

But the fact that art is rooted in collective experience is not simply an established fact, a secondary characteristic which one might assume 'in addition' to artistic creation. It is an essential part of the very life of a work of art, and only through ignorance or dishonesty can these two factors be separated.

Since the work of art exists in relation to the outlook of a certain period, group or individual and is found in types of society having different experiences of human relationships and emotions, it is necessary, in order to measure the depth to which imagined creation is rooted in society, to define these factors both in relation to artistic attitudes, either known or implied, and in relation to the function exercised by art in a particular type of society.

At the point of intersection between the *creative attitudes* and the *functions* of art in different structures – that is the starting point for a sociology of artistic creation. We propose, therefore, to examine the various aesthetic attitudes in history and the diversity of functions exercised by imagined creation in different social structures.

The Variety of Aesthetic Attitudes

Yes, 'art' is indeed dead – but a little investigation will show how many aesthetic attitudes can exist together in the same period, even when the period officially calls for a single 'style' of expression.

These attitudes describe the original contexts which correspond to whatever the artist represents in his work and to whatever he inspires in his contemporaries, as well as to the way in which he justifies his own work to himself and to others like him, and to the ideologies which he claims to hold and to the techniques which he employs. However, these attitudes bear no resemblance to partial representations, even if they are highly intellectualized. Rather, these attitudes establish the way in which man relates to the imaginary and in which he sees himself in relation to the ideals which reach beyond the trivial scope of everyday life. To a certain extent these attitudes can be likened to an 'intuition of values', in the sense that Max Scheler uses the phrase, although without implying an accompanying ontology or dogmatism. Their 'transcendence' is still within the bounds of real experience, however far it represents an effort to expand.

It is, then, an attempt at re-arrangement, because such attitudes can offer a new pattern of aesthetic and social signs, suggestive of some hypothetical unity between them. But since contemporary society will be unfamiliar with this new unity, which must always remain 'only an idea', perpetually ahead of the time when it is conceived, style creates a collective and individual *expectancy*. In *The Critique of Judgement*, Kant states that aesthetic judgement always assumes an 'as if', and appears as a judgement which has the power perpetually to entrance us, even if we are continually aware of it. Sociology can interpret this suggestion by perceiving in the *attitude* an effort, transcending immediate experience, to establish a community where human contact could be absolute, where signs would be unnecessary because man's consciousness would be so completely liberated that he would no longer need to use symbols for the purpose of communication. This is not a mere dream, however, because these attitudes, within the context of actual collective life, are continually searching for suitable social structures.

It is this continual search for social structures which gives these attitudes their validity in sociological terms. They do not add up to 'visions of the world', with all that implies of a logical, ontological foundation; nor are they merely psychological patterns of behaviour which can be reduced to an emotional level of experience. These attitudes attempt to create a 'society'. It is in this way that the imaginary plays its true part within the framework of social life.

However – and this probably fixes the limits of artistic experience in relation to other social experiences of men – these 'attitudes' are few in number and can be found again and again, in various guises and at various stages of development, in most societies. Whether or not they are strongly developed, and whether or not they are highly rationalized, such attitudes represent the many different functions man has attributed to art. It is only recently, for reasons which will be clear at the end of our investigation, that these re-current attitudes have given way to completely new and un-precedented ones.

The first attitude we shall study corresponds to the similarity which exists between social and aesthetic experi-ence, when systems of classification and symbols meet at a certain level of intensity within the variable and changing dynamism of collective life itself.

In fact, this attitude to art, which we might call an *aesthetic of total communion*, implies above all an absence of what nowadays we consider as 'art'. It involves a relation-ship between the signs advanced by an individual (who may be chosen in the same way as a 'sorcerer') and a human group. The signs of expression only acquire meaning if what the artist signifies refers to something which becomes immediately significant and has symbolic value for the group which receives and registers it. The resulting alliance between art and society is so close that on the occasion of public festivals or seasonal rituals there is a quite unique and instant identification between the two. These festivals become the means of achieving such an identification which, although sought everywhere, is only possible in the context of such public occasions. This is so for several reasons: dis-persal of population and a lack of what Durkheim calls 'social density'; absence of (or weak) division of labour; the fact that public occasions with their 'effervescent environ-ment' are usually determined by ecological and geograph-ical conditions and by the natural forces which surround and dominate the entire society. The symbolism of such occasions is immediately perceptible to the entire group (in a way which can momentarily remove the weak social groupings) and is identified with the experience of every member.

In addition, a fundamental characteristic of these 'com-munions' intensified by signs (which only now do we label as artistic) is that they exclude not only the written word but all forms of language which do not use a vocabulary common to all and understood by all. We can understand, therefore, why this attitude to art normally finds its expression in dramatic terms, whether formal or informal.[41]

Historically speaking, the point of attribution of these 'communions' created by art is diverse. Sometimes it can be located in what we call 'primitive or archaic societies' (which in fact were not 'simple' at all); sometimes one finds it deeply rooted in nascent urban societies, such as those which precede powerful rural, feudal or patriarchal civilizations, as for example in Greece at the moment when liturgical drama was replaced by Aeschylean drama,[42] or again in Japan at the moment when Zeami codified another type of historical drama, the Nō theatre, which, because of a respect for tradition and strict rules, had become dormant and paralysed.[43]

In this situation man presents an image of man for other men, but not 'man' in the sense in which we or humanists use the word. Here man is a dual *masked* being whose hidden, troubled side is generally condemned or mutilated, at the same time as it is affirmed, even if guiltily. This is man who appears before the spectator with his past like a retinue trailing behind him; he can no more shake himself free from it than Orestes could shake off the dreadful power of the Furies. Besides, we can recognize this distress and misery. They are what a culture designates as the very image of terror and fear. Those who express this distress and misery appear to be almost creating them, but in fact these emotions still belonged to everyone, even when they are concentrated in a guilty hero such as Prometheus. In reality, what is portrayed are people and not characters.

However, the actual value of this attitude has been overrated. The failure to locate it properly in its points of precise attribution ('archaic' societies, the first manifestations of urban societies) has meant that it has inspired the kind of aesthetic reveries we associate with Rousseau or Nietzsche.

68

When Rousseau in *Considérations sur le gouvernement de Pologne* refers to 'public games', those festivals during which the people as a whole dramatize their own existence (a passage which was used almost word for word at the time of the French Revolution as an inspiration for its 'civic festivals'), the author of *The Social Contract* was thinking of closed, confined societies, separated from the rest of the world by a religion or by some common belief – the kind of society, in fact, in which he himself grew up in his own native Protestant Geneva. When Nietzsche compared Greek theatre in its classical phase with its later period when it was divided and dispersed by conflicting theories, and then suggested that only the early theatre could have produced authentic tragedy, he too was deceived by the illusion of a closely-knit, fraternal community.

In fact, the aesthetic 'communion' that we are speaking of, in which symbols and the objects symbolized fuse together physically in a momentary oneness – usually in dance or in diverse dramatic forms – appears only in extremely limited circumstances. Neither the historian nor the sociologist can allow such a specific attitude to be generalized.

Nevertheless, this unattainable fraternity does give rise to a valid creative attitude, but in the form of a *nostalgia for a lost communion*, an impossible dream kept alive by man's undying wish for emotional unity. In Europe and Japan (the only two regions of the world which, before the beginning of the twentieth century, had made the transition from a traditional to an industrial type of society), this attitude is expressed by the visions of Schiller, Goethe, Hölderlin, Nietzsche (all dreaming of the lost world of Greece), of Hugo and Wagner (inspired by the legends of the Middle Ages); and by the nostalgia among the Japanese artists who looked back to 'the great past' (even in modern cinema, with the 'Samurai' films).* The reason for this frustration

* The same underlying nostalgia is found in Pasternak's *Doctor Zhivago*. The hero is trying to find a fraternal bond with the Revolu-

is that these societies have become increasingly diversified and stratified, divided by the necessity for professional specialization and organized into castes and classes. In such societies, unity can only be achieved within sects, that is, small and inevitably artificial and discordant groups, within theatres which provoke a passive and momentary participation, and within groups of young people who, through the violence and rhythm of music and dance, escape from the demands of a highly diversified society.* However, we stress the fact that this nostalgia is not caused by recognizing that even in an industrial society, whether developing or established, there is a possibility of achieving reconciliation. It is provoked by the atomization of man's life which is the irreversible outcome of man's commitment to a technological world, with all the individual suffering it brings.

This attitude is *romantic* in the real sense of the word. And it has been encouraged by Winckelmann, by the discovery of ancient cities, by the widespread exploitation of ruins, and even recently by the aesthetics of Malraux. In order to specify more clearly the point of attribution of this attitude to social life, it is necessary to say that this nostalgia is always twofold: that which is inherent in modern societies at the moment when they cast off their traditions, and that which goes with a powerlessness to intervene effectively in social life. Thus, it was in a Germany suffering from the sclerosis of ageing institutions, but fully aware of the significance of political and economic revolutions in France and England, that there arose a disturbing nostalgia for a lost world, a yearning in which the poet's signs and their effect

tion and, failing to do so, seeks it in love and in religious faith. I have discussed this idea in an article in *Arguments*.

* It is in this sense (and not from an 'official' standpoint) that we must interpret certain activities of younger people, whether dealing with the 'bus palladium', happenings or collective demonstrations by Dutch provos.

on his public are infused with the same passionate sense of brotherhood.

One can also see how this frustration can become creative in a stratified society where art tries to recreate a past unity, either by expecting melody or *leitmotiv* (Wagner) to provide a non-intellectualized image of feelings and of inner life, an image which absorbs everyone and destroys the barriers between them; or by expecting myth (verbal, poetic, recited, written, dramatized) to bring about an otherwise impossible harmony. Myth, which is necessarily primitive, cannot bring about this unity of awareness, because in the society which produces this aesthetic attitude, men are divided and separated from one another by social barriers, by different interests, by political ideologies; and these barriers are far more difficult to break down than those which separate one 'primitive' culture from another.*

* We can surely see the phenomenon of Hitler's national socialism as one of the points of attribution of this attitude to art, but in this case not associated with a truly original creative background, but rather abandoned to itself and allowed to fall into the hands of neurotic, self-made men. The desire to re-establish a spiritual unanimity which will overcome impregnable class barriers by creating intense participation in the context of ceremonies, military parades where music, noise, rhythm, action and flags automatically produce a common enthusiasm in which all the groups present merge into one mass – all these things (intellectualized with uneven success by Alfred Rosenberg's *Der Mythus des 20. Jahrhunderts* and Hitler's *Mein Kampf*) go towards creating a total unity called 'the nation' where a kind of communion is sought as forcefully and racially as in small and scattered ancient societies.

But in Germany we have a highly industrialized society, a society where classes and castes strongly defend social barriers; unanimity on a level of practical politics here takes the form of a 'blood religion', racism and military massing of men. No one can overcome the obstacle of class divisions, nor without terrorism can anyone apply the forms valid for one type of society to the narrow dimensions of a radically different type of society. This illustrates the way in which an attitude to art can react quite differently on a certain social environment and turn into an active ideology.

To a certain extent, Hitlerism was both the triumph and the final defeat of an attitude which dominated every aspect of public and

The third aesthetic attitude recognizable in history and in many different human societies is similar to the preceding one, since in this attitude art is identified with religion or, more precisely, with the sacred, although in actual fact it is completely different from it.

We are now dealing with charismatic societies where the artist becomes *the priest of the absolute*, the earthly representative of God, of the sacred or of the power which dispenses a higher law. The artist is seen as a wise man or prophet, and whatever he produces is consecrated; everything is absorbed into this mediation which gives the artist a supernatural power, often confused with that of the priest or a divine.

However, it is necessary to distinguish between art which expresses religious feelings, and art imbued with the spirituality which is inseparable from it. Malraux mentions this important distinction and indicates that a separation takes place at the level of the relationship between artists and form: that the artist lets himself be 'fascinated' by 'primordial forms' which brings us to Lagash's figures or to Sumerian art at Tello; that the artist *suggests* a religious fervour by expressing his own separate consciousness, which brings us to Christian or Buddhist sculpture.[44]

This important distinction can only be related to these famous 'primordial forms' when, at the level of creative experience, we find a *super-human* desire to sanctify the figurative representation, as in Sumerian and Aztec art, and a desire to *humanize* them, as in Roman or Buddhist art. The 'primordial' element in these forms depends on the deliberately unreal – because greatly simplified – presence of prehistoric figures in which human and non-human signs

---

private life, in the sense that men like Stefan Georg or Gabriele D'Annunzio envisaged it well before Nazism became a reality (for this reason we cannot simply consider them responsible, so childish was their dream). I have tried to analyse this subject more closely, but in the particular field of the novel in *L'Or de la république* (Paris, 1957).

are combined. Yet these 'primordial forms' are not like this *because* they are 'primordial', but because they combine two levels of the systems of classification – one based on the life of the community, the other on nature. These images only inspire panic and terror because they express encounters or give a religious meaning to confrontations.

These two aspects of the sacred in art show the fullness of experience which is found in many countries, not only among the charismatic oriental societies (Chaldaea, ancient Egypt, the Inca empire), but also in most feudal societies divided into a caste system like those of the European Middle Ages or those of the period of the Vedas in India. In the first case, the artist, acting as the intercessor (generally unknown and unknowable), is confused with the 'fetish maker', as has been suggested was the case in Egypt: he represents the signs of the most intense kind of communion, at least during the earlier dynasties.[45] What we call the representation of daily life, what naively appears to us as 'realism', is in fact a theophanic effort to justify this life and to exalt our progress through the world, under the eye of hidden powers awaiting us after death. What we experience, perhaps, before the feeding of King Thutmose III by the goddess Isis, represented by a sycamore tree, is a peculiarly modern feeling; but this naked figure, drawn like one of Klee's figures in the middle of a tree with simple leaf-shapes, only indirectly relates to our modern feelings. The goddess embodies, at the highest level, the spiritualization of earthly forms which inspires this encounter (here represented imaginatively) between natural classifications (the tree) and human classifications (the king).[46]

It is a question of the intensification of life by a force which swamps, overpowers, elevates and finally judges it. This is not realism. 'One should understand,' writes an Egyptologist, 'that in Egypt a beautiful monument was defined as an *efficient work* (*menekh*).'[47] This puts an end to any hope of finding a naturalistic source in the experience which turns the imaginary form into an act directed towards God and which unites a society around its own fears.

Another aspect of this 'sanctifying' attitude appears in Roman art, in Byzantine and Buddhist painters, and in the sacred plays of the Middle Ages in Europe. The attitude does not reflect a particular spirituality, but *interprets* religious activity in societies where religious hierarchies, having become strongly organized in institutions and groups of all kinds, begin to compete with other social hierarchies. In societies like those of European countries in the Middle Ages (where competition between social groups was as intense as the factions involved were numerous), the forms of human expression represent the sacred as an aggressive and persuasive force. Certainly, Christian values strengthened European 'civilization'; but these values were *represented* as values – that is to say, as models to be realized – by a Church which had its part to play in a complex society, although it did not identify itself with that society. This important distinction between the beliefs common to everyone and an 'institution' whose claims to universality were far from being recognized, makes it clear that religion had to *play the part of* or represent the destiny of man on earth, in order to inspire the intellectual and emotional allegiance which in reality could not be assumed. This produces the intensity and richness of sculptured figures and architecture which, as H. Focillon has shown, were a *language*, and the *views* implied in them corresponded to an attempt to invest the space of society with a sacred space.[48] This cannot be understood if one accepts the unity of the spiritual and social life in the Middle Ages, as one still did only fifty years ago.

Whether these figures express encounters between natural and social classifications, whether they capture in the face of an individual an intense spiritual experience which gives proof of a religious conflict presupposed by everyone, or whether it is a question of *spectacular* dramatizations, the same illusion is aimed at. Men had to be integrated into a spiritual framework in order to restore to the Church the totality of souls that were contained in free urban communities, numerous monarchies still too weak to be centralizing forces, bodies of traders and workmen.[49]

But whatever aspect is assumed by this attitude which confuses sacred art with the sacred, it remains a very particular expression and in no way covers the wide range of creativity. This is an added confirmation of the enormous variety of human experiences, in which the sacred in all its forms only occupies a place of limited importance.

Another aesthetic attitude, embedded in different types of society, can be called *the deliberate illustration of everyday life*. This attitude has been seen as the culmination of an effort, the 'progress from the simple nobility of self-communion and contemplation to an increasing secularization', as Hegel says.[50] Certainly, it is unfortunate not to feel the beauty of the 'moment' or the 'long Sunday of life which smoothes out all problems and lies beyond the reach of all corruption' that Hegel describes. But we would question the philosopher's presupposition which identifies 'comfortable, middle-class life' with the determination to illustrate that life. Is this not to confuse the explanation with what should be explained?

Nevertheless, Hegel is perfectly justified in making a definite link between this attitude to art and a social group, because such an attitude depends on the vitality which can only be found in an organization of men held together by common interest; but he is wrong to make it the exclusive right of the middle class or indeed of any class. It has existed in other types of society, of castes or of groups which were not classes, and which also managed to sublimate everyday life, in all its transitory or permanent aspects, in all its unusual, momentary or unexpected encounters – like the Persians in the great period of Chiraz, Japanese Zen painters and Chinese artists.

In this case the group is looking at itself in a mirror, and it uses the system of classification on which its economic activity is based (as in Holland), its equilibrium, its momentary security (Persia) to provide a means of exaltation, of contentment, of comfort, of consolidation and of confirmation, in order to support its way of life, its 'destiny'. Ultimately, one might be able to speak of a personal sublimation of a particular way of life, of establishing a defence which will guarantee a group's survival, particularly when it is threatened by other groups or is simply condemned by time.

This attitude can be found, for example, among the privileged castes of the Roman Empire, who, in mosaics, in murals and statues created an everyday world which was an enchanted double of the real world. We find this same heightening of daily life in Chinese painting of the T'ang Dynasty, when the painter, by now well-educated, abandons the *tao* (the Zen way towards the discovery of fundamental essences through figurative representation) in favour of portraying real experience,[51] and in the Dutch Reform principalities, founded on trade and surrounded by centralizing Catholic monarchies. In the case of the latter we really see an effort to place the social group within a certain framework; to prolong life by representing it in order to overcome the fear of inescapable isolation, and to enhance an unexciting environment by instituting it as the only one possible in the eyes of those who are surrounded by it – as though it was a secret garden. But this secret garden is a prison, a ghetto which shelters a way of life unsure of its own continuation, which it can only preserve by persuading itself that the world resembles it and that it is unique in the world. The middle classes in France and England also adopted this attitude when they reacted against 'noble' values which had nevertheless inspired them for centuries; they set up their own ethic of honesty and virtue, a value based on nature and goodness which is found in Diderot and is affirmed to a greater degree in the eighteenth-century English novel. Many examples of these tendencies are given by Groethuysen in *Origines de l'esprit bourgeois en France*.

Later, in the Victorian era, we again find this tendency re-affirmed, but there it was additionally limited to the experience of a caste which held all the economic and political power. This caste used the attitude to affirm its determination to rise above the trivial values of commerce and business by exalting the moral dignity of official life. Likewise, during the Stalin period in Russia, the need to represent working life was naturally assumed, but it was a working life planned and reconstructed by a small powerful élite, who not only fixed the norms of work and of daily life but also the image of the 'ideal citizen'. 'Socialist realism,' as it was conceived at that time, also involved the establishment of an aesthetic ghetto where Soviet man could find confirmation of his difficult and threatened existence.

Clearly, this attitude can be rooted in social structures which are very different but which always imply a similar situation: that of a caste, of a group or a class, which sometimes is imprisoned by the very image it creates of its own life, and which sometimes prolongs a daily life that it would like to magnify.

It would be tempting, but wrong, to confuse this attitude which illustrates daily life with another aesthetic attitude which we can find in history, which can be called *the art of reservations or of closed doors*. However, there are obvious differences between the ambitions of an active group, which is economically and socially confined to a small area, and the often esoteric entertainment arranged by priests and educated men for their own pleasure. It is true that when, in time, definite social particularities disappear, the secret side of this kind of art vanishes with them, with the result that subsequent eras give it an importance which it was far from possessing in its time.

The best example of this attitude can be found in the intellectual drama conceived, written and acted by and for clerics during the Middle Ages in Europe and the Renaissance – the plays of Rhoswita, the nun of Magdeburg, the plays translated or adapted from Terence (which in editions released by early printers had great influence), and the plays of pre-Shakespearian 'university-wits'. We would also include under this heading all the art and literary productions of Roman society, excessively over-valued by the universities, and which, at the time, only survived as entertainment reserved for those aristocrats who could afford to keep scribes, painters and poets.

In order to define the exact conditions to which this attitude belonged, we need only keep the meanings which were used by the artists themselves, because their work was produced against a general background of illiteracy and 'barbarity', and also because the only people who had the power or the right to communicate thought were usually found among artists or were artists themselves. This was just what happened in the case of the clerics of the Middle Ages, and the Roman or Chinese scholars who made themselves the sole protectors of 'culture' and who devoted their 'leisure' activity to so high and noble an awareness that their beliefs became universal and absolute. Indeed, these enclosed circles of artists, protected by patrons or by a religious or political power, generally created their own language – a language of prisoners in a system of values – which then spread out beyond the narrow framework in which they were confined. 'We clerics' or 'we artists' became 'we men'. The many definitions which have been given to humanism before the nineteenth century originate from nothing other than this interpretation.

We should not conclude from this that the forms of expression corresponding to this attitude are unproductive or second-rate. In the hot-house atmosphere of clerical and esoteric gatherings, there survived a practice of the arts which otherwise would have died out. The Academies which developed in Italian cities of the _Quattrocento_ have been discussed elsewhere:[52] it was in the midst of these groups of scholars and artists that the new classifications of the human order were formed which later were crystallized in the ideas of Alberti and in the work of Leonardo da Vinci. But it would be wrong to imagine that the Academies were open, or that a large public audience attended the debates on subjects which only today have become 'universal'. It was behind closed doors that the doctrines were worked out.

The translations or Latin productions of Seneca's plays (important as they were for the development of European drama) were never staged for the general public, only for clerical audiences. It is quite possible that the theatre would not have progressed beyond the stage it had reached at that time – when it was an esoteric form of entertainment for intellectuals – if the groups of scholars had continued to assume that dramatic creation belonged exclusively to them, as in fact happened to the Japanese Nō theatre which, codified by the school of Zeami, never went on to tackle tragic themes or others generally performed in the theatre.

Such a devoted following, such aristocratic cliques possessing energy and fortune, the attitudes peculiar to them – these can all be found in many types of society. Sometimes these cliques flourish, sometimes they die out because they are sterile as all such esoteric, intellectual groups inevitably are. Usually, they develop their own language, their own systems of values and, when their activities do not follow the direction which others take, they cling obstinately to their own enthusiasms. Patronage and snobbery do not always need a court society or an active monarchy, such as we find under Louis XIV, nor even 'salons', such as Proust frequented and in which major political events of the day had their repercussions.

The very worst that can happen is for aesthetic activity to turn in on itself, to consume itself, or to fan the flames of its own destruction. The poet or artist, in this case, lives in a kind of reservation, like the American Indian. His language is that of an in-group, whose main preoccupation is to foster the image it has of its own superiority and isolation. This is a way of protecting oneself against real life, a way of safe-guarding one's own values from danger. At times, this with-drawal can help the seeds of creativity to survive periods of social chaos or military rule, as, for instance, in China after the Manchurian conquest. At times like this, these 'reserva-tions' keep a 'night watch' which protects the disciplines of an art which it is temporarily impossible to practise. But at other times, these 'reservations' become shelters for nourishing rarefied pedantic concerns in an artificial peace and calm.

Another attitude, much more widespread and active be-cause it relies on the efforts of small groups striving for political power and social dominance, can be called *art as expenditure of wealth*. In this situation, the imaginary has to yield up sumptuous, exotic works of art, offered either to God or to other men, who are required or ordered to make an *exchange* in which they can only participate if they give their approval and applause.

The traveller in Latin America finds examples every-where of that gigantic *potlatch* made to God in the form of churches and statues, as offerings from the wealth of the land. Churches such as those of Ouro Preto in the state of Minas Gerais in Brazil, the church of San Bento de Rio and the convent of Tepoztotlan in Mexico, are all outstanding examples of that energy displayed at the time of the con-quest of America and of the establishment of a European settlement on the other side of the Atlantic. Need we be reminded that these aesthetic forms, loaded with gold and riches, are an indication of the emotional turmoil of the first explorers? This is not the place for us to go deeply into something which might make us re-question all that is generally accepted about baroque art; let us simply bear in mind that it is not just a question of an energy and a spirit. As both Pierre Francastel and Pierre Charpentrat have suggested,[53] one can define the movement as a social practice, a mode of behaviour, a living attitude closely connected with a particular milieu. This milieu is not only (as was the case in Central Europe in the area where the baroque movement was influential) associated with a violent change taking place in the traditional ways of life; in Latin America it involved a sumptuous consummation, an exalted kind of debauchery inseparable from the discovery of gold and new lands, often to the terror of the aboriginal civilizations.

These Brazilian, Peruvian and Mexican sculptured figures are dedicated to God, as are the prolific and better executed figures in Central Europe. But they have been overloaded with a prodigious abundance. Disdainful of gold because of his religious beliefs, and yet fascinated by its richness and the worldly power this metal confers on him, man has tried to undertake a mighty auto-da-fé. Is it not a matter of attracting the attention of God, of trying to get Him to exchange divine grace for human gifts? Is it surprising that men should barter with God, that they should try to draw Him into the endless business of loaning on interest – gifts in exchange for grace? One can only imagine the terrible anguish which must have driven artists and patrons, the intense expectancy which must have led them into such debaucheries of creation and extravagance. Does not the violent passion which is considered to be the principal characteristic of the Baroque spring from man's anxiety as he awaits a response from God? When Alejadino created the statues of Congonhas de Campo or the fantastic figures which fill the churches of Ouro Preto, when the Jesuits took the sons of the conquered Aztec princes, whom they educated, to work with them on the ornate wall decorations of the Abbey of Tepoztotlan, were they not beginning a dialogue whose outcome they would never know? In this case, does not art spring from the doubts in man, who makes gifts to God, uncertain of whether or not there will be any response?

Gifts presented to men are no less sumptuous. Perhaps one faction or a family wishes to dominate others, as in Venice or Florence; perhaps a prince or emperor decides to spend the spoils of conquest and plunder on public spectacles, like the Roman games; or perhaps the aristocracy of a town wishes to master its own people, as for example in the centralizing monarchies which sprang up in the fifteenth and sixteenth centuries in Italy, France, England and Germany.

In every case, a prince with the help of his artists begins to vie with another in giving presents, then draws him into a contest of sumptuous exchanges, forcing him to respond with further gifts, and, when the other can give no more, demands the recognition of his own superiority. The Field of the Cloth of Gold and the 'royal parades' of the Renaissance are evidence of this custom.[54] In this way, the sovereign makes his people aware of his own prestige by contrasting it with the inferiority of other men who cannot make the necessary gifts – the man in the street, the artisan, the 'bourgeoisie' – or with the inferiority of the other rulers, who must reply to his gift with their allegiance. Public holidays, architectural decorations, an abundance of plastic creations, either lasting or occasional (artists' workshops equalled the courts of the princes in rivalry), public performances spectacularly staged – this exchange ensured a rapid and highly effective circulation of values and symbols.

It is not necessary to look elsewhere to find the 'climate' of what we have called the Renaissance; it cannot be explained in terms of a religion of individualism, nor as a return to antiquity, nor as the emergence from a 'dark age', nor the discovery of 'enlightenment'. All these factors can only be understood by means of that powerful *rivalry* among creative forms which is played out in a common, essentially urban setting, and which is the result of the subtle interplay of exchanges – gifts made and accepted for real or symbolic purposes. The setting up of centralizing monarchies and the increasing importance of economic factors in societies undoubtedly limited this extravagant exchange of gifts and presents, restricting it to the enclosed space of a palace or of a château, and before long, of a theatre.*

At the time of the Reformation in Europe, this aesthetic attitude was a distinguishing factor between Catholicism and Protestantism. The Reformers protested against the splendour of buildings in Rome, and of St Peter's in particular (as events show, at least), and they refused to participate in offering so much *potlatch* to God. Instead, they sought to interiorize faith as one might interiorize riches by accumulating them. But the dichotomy established by Max Weber is not sufficiently flexible: Catholicism in Spain, in Portugal and in Venice offered to God or to men an artistic *potlatch*, and Venetian extravagance is an eulogy of the richness of the universe, intensified perhaps by eastern influences on the Catholic city of the Doges, who were themselves already somewhat byzantine in outlook. The Reformers despised such external displays and even banned the theatre, as happened under Puritan rule in England; but the influence of Protestantism was not so wretchedly restrictive in every country. The gap between those who hoarded gold out of scorn for it (whether Catholics or Reformers), and those who displayed their faith by offering their wealth to God, in the [form of gifts, became increasingly wider. Anxiety and disquiet were felt not only by the man who believed in hoarding riches, even though his belief in predestination and grace hardly left his personal happiness open to chance. No, anxiety was also felt, perhaps more

* The rivalry between Fouquet and the young Louis XIV was at first expressed with a *potlatch* of festivals, but the king quickly stopped the exchanges from going any further. He was not one to give interest on loans.

so, by the man trying to persuade himself of the existence of God, trying, even at the expense of his own material ruin, to make God descend to earth. Has the intense drama of that time in Spain and Portugal ever been fully appreciated? Gold poured in from America in increasing abundance, but on the roads out of Ouro Preto or from the Inca temples huge churches were being built, each one of them the embodiment of the questions that man was asking about himself. Finally, the gold arrived in the hands of the two conquering nations, and then found its way to Flanders and England, and into the money-chests of men for whom open expression of life meant less than the silent and wearying struggle of the conscience to justify itself. And when that openly displayed faith was confronted by the strange unknown world of dead or dying civilizations in the new continents of America, there were no limits to its frightened determination to assert itself, and, through imagined representation, to project the image of a faith which was becoming more desperate, the more it dramatized itself.

The Baroque has been discussed so much that its essential feature which is directly connected with religious and economic activities, has been forgotten. The desperation expressed in art forms corresponds to the more generous giving of gifts, to a stronger appeal, to an increasingly impatient magical invocation to draw the divine down into everyday life and into the vale of tears in which men live. The art of statuary, of the theatre (Cervantes, Lope and Calderón's last 'autos sacramentales') and of architecture were all dominated by the resolute determination to magnify and increase the gift presented to God, so as to entice Him into the labyrinth of human exchanges and to involve Him again in a world which He seemed to be disdaining, and which in fact He only disdained in the eyes of those who interiorized their faith. This intense frustration was being felt all over Europe at the time when capitalism was forcing Europe into the modern age.

But this determination to create striking displays can be found in other societies and at other moments of history which were not so dominated by religion or mysticism. Then the sole concern was the desire to gain a response to the gift which art enhanced, and to provoke a *potlatch* which justified every passion, every embellishment. This is what the prince in Florence or in Italian towns during the *Trecento* was aiming at when he sent a procession of poets and painted or sculptured figures through the streets. Similarly, this was the aim of the Roman emperor who used to invite the populace to the spectacular displays of a circus, at a time when violence and cruelty had replaced the passion for art. Again, in our own time, this is the aim of 'world fairs' in certain liberal societies where art is associated with technology, so perceptively analysed by Francastel.[55] It is also the aim of certain forms of contemporary cinema, the 'epic' film, for example. All of these are examples of a comparable aesthetic determination.

Another aesthetic attitude, which became highly important in Europe at the time when the impact of modern economic developments was being felt (and which can be found in ancient times and also in Japan during the Meiji era), can be described as *the opposition on ethical grounds to the traditional culture of society and to its established values.*

This opposition has been badly misunderstood. Too often it is regarded as a kind of literary 'rebellion' or romantic anarchism, when in fact it is a profoundly creative attitude, proposing a schemata of behaviour, the potentialities of inter-human relationships and, in total, a matrix of particular forms which are in conflict with the established norms of a society no longer interested in change.

This attitude has two distinct components. One is upheld in the transition from one type of society to another which logically follows it; the other implies that the type of society which tends to replace the earlier one does not exclude an awareness of a burdensome past, neither the survival of existing institutions, nor the 'intuition' (in the sense in which Scheler uses the word) of new values, nor the presentiment of ways of life, as yet unknown but made necessary because of man's adaptation to fresh situations.

These interruptions in continuity cannot always be observed with the same accuracy, and we have already put forward the hypothesis that creative periods of art accompany such changes and follow them, either closely, or at a distance. Particularly in the arts which are capable of explicit protest (literature and the theatre), that is to say, which speak the language of collective consciousness, the opposition to traditional values becomes the driving force behind all creativity – a force which is concealed but undoubtedly present.

The theatre did not originate simply as a re-arrangement of liturgical pageants, or as popular adaptations of classical works for the public of a later age. Orestes takes on himself the guilt of a crime committed in the name of a 'vendetta' which the city had outlawed, and must appear before its symbolic representative to obtain pardon. Antigone performs an old patriarchal rite which the laws of the town have banned and, innocent criminal that she is, makes her distress public without winning sympathy – she is regarded as an unreal, transitory relic of the recent past. Tamberlaine, murderer and criminal, appears on the English stage and with his crimes opens the way to Elizabethan drama, not to mention European theatre. He is the first in a long line of murderous kings whom Shakespeare and Fletcher, after Marlowe, bring to life.

Such apparently negative values are not however unproductive. They express opposition to the traditional order, either by unmasking the face of crime (Prometheus, Antigone, Orestes) or by showing that the old order inhibits any possible development in human relationships (for example, the 'feud' which separates Romeo and Juliet, or

Rodrigue and Chimène in *Le Cid*). Perhaps the dramatist makes the power of the old order appear to be in the right; nevertheless, it is the opposition, the conflict, the protest, which sanctions the confrontation between the old values and those which herald the future. Without that opposition, there would be no tragedy, and no literature either.

It is true that this kind of violence, these ambiguous protests against the established order, constitute what Antonin Artaud has called 'the theatre of cruelty',[56] but in themselves they are relatively minor factors; they are not all that the artist expresses and his work does not depend on them alone. As we have said, he can represent them ambiguously so that it is impossible to judge whether he regrets or condemns them. But even more so, he needs to evoke their very opposite. This is the vital dialectical process which operates in a creative work: to the suffering caused by adhesion to the old rules, to which are attached more crimes than are associated with the emerging society, the artist, and especially the dramatist, introduces a nostalgia for peace and compromise.

One cannot help seeing here, in this nostalgia for harmony, an early form of humanism. At the end of Shakespeare's *Macbeth*, the victorious king, after a brief reflection over the dead body of his enemy, whose death avenges so many crimes, goes 'to be crowned at Scone'. But it will not be long before the new king will himself be cruel and tyrannical. Thus the infernal cycle goes on, for power can never be permanently established. Similarly, in Lope de Vega and in Corneille, it is a king who intervenes and puts an end to the 'vendetta' or to the injustices of the feudal overlords. This intervention undoubtedly results from uncertainty on the part of the dramatist, who, on the one hand, is faced with the values of a disappearing world, and on the other with relationships which another world could establish among men, if its development were not hindered by a lifeless system.

However, the forms which this aesthetic attitude assumes do not always correspond to disruptions which interfere with the continuity of social life. Over a period of time, societies develop a particular character which is built up by accumulating events and collective expectations directed towards a common end, so justifying the establishment of a more rigid system of values. This process of development can take place either in social consciousness, that is, historically and chronologically, or else below the level of consciousness where it cannot be documented. Nonetheless, this process takes place *within* a certain type of society and the presuppositions on which the active existence of that society is based. When disruption occurs, and a new type of society begins to develop within the boundaries of the old (leaving aside the kind of total disruption and extinction which was inflicted on Carthage by the Romans), the values on which the order and existence of the old world were founded cease to be desirable and wholesome and become inflexible prescriptions and exigencies, which seem all the more stringent because they no longer correspond to an actual human environment. At this point, new values (as yet undefined) are sought – simple inner needs or directions, aspirations, attempts towards new emotions. Such expectations constitute one of the fundamental elements in the historical transition from one society to another, and also form the most primitive elements in man's anticipation of what is to come – an anticipation whose forms are necessarily imaginary. Nevertheless, this anticipation creates in man a painful, and often tragic or desperate, tension between what he wants to achieve and what his existence offers him in reality; this is because he is prevented from developing his potential beyond the limitations imposed by traditional values. We are aware of only one aspect of this opposition, that which is represented by the imaginary figure who symbolizes something which has not yet materialized, and which perhaps never will, in the way that the unresolved image of freedom and human advancement, as presented by Marlowe or Corneille, has never become reality for any man.

These imagined figures (either in the theatre or the novel) are necessarily ambivalent: on the one hand, they are characters who are immoderate (Defoe's *Moll Flanders* and *Lady Roxana*), paradoxical (*Le Neveu de Rameau*), anguished (*René* or *Werther*) or prey to desperate ambitions (Julien Sorel); on the other hand, they reconcile the differences which separate two eras, and soothe the conflicts which cause more suffering in the person who fights against them than in the instigators. We have tried to show elsewhere how this tension, at an individual level, tends to intensify in the period in Europe between the advent of the age of commerce and the political revolutions of the nineteenth century. Whereas Marlowe and Shakespeare were able to assert their 'differences', Lenz, Kleist, Hölderlin and Nerval turned against themselves the overwhelming menace and violence which were implied. It was perhaps their own recognition that the tension could never be resolved, that there was no escape from it, which lay at the heart of their suicidal madness.[57]

In each case, it is a question of an ethical opposition to old values, to a 'culture' which is seen to be decadent, and which is in the process of disappearing to make way for another culture, which only exists symbolically, momentarily lacking in significance.* This enables us to see to what extent artistic creation is involved in the existential framework of collective life, and to what extent it responds to the expectations and demands revealed by men during periods of change, because it acts as a mirror or a schema of a free-

* We do not include in this the kind of 'philistinism' which claims to see changes which do not exist. It is easy to say 'a new age is beginning' and remain foolishly tied to ideas belonging to the past. Real visions of the future are not based on 'intellectual notions'; they rationalize our fears and, above all, the immense realm of the unaccomplished, still to be lived out.

dom which seeks through (or in spite of) old determinisms to suggest new relationships between men. If these new relationships are no more worthwhile than those which have already been standardized by habit and stagnation, they at least have the virtue of being different.

This does not mean that these potentialities, symbolized in characters, can always materialize into fact. Basically they are presentiments, undeveloped by living outlines, which propose an *eventual* experience. Does this not explain why the great characters of the novel and of the theatre – such as Robinson Crusoe, Julien Sorel, Hamlet or Faust – in time become symbols?

A variant of this attitude is expressed by the revolt of art in growing industrial societies – for instance, the political and romantic revolt of Vigny, Byron or Wagner against the inevitably commercial world in which they found themselves immersed. Perhaps the radical changes in people's lives, caused by the concentration of population in industrial towns at the beginning of the nineteenth century, played an important part in confirming this attitude in the minds of the general public.[58] The 'myth of Paris', the 'myth of the working-class', the 'myth of the underdog' or the myth of a society in which the man who thinks and writes (the 'intellectual') is the Caesar, the Napoleon – these are all variants of the same attitude.[59] Both melodrama of the kind that portrayed crime in the streets and, later, the cinema gathered up the seeds of this attitude and developed them for a much larger public.

All this is possible for the simple reason that the expression which corresponds most often to this attitude, at least in Europe and in Japan,* involves the formation of a

---

* These at present are the only parts of the world (we include the USA and Canada in Europe by virtue of their inherited civilization and culture) where the old world has developed completely into the modern capitalist age. The 'Third World' (including South America) is still on the threshold of economic revolution.

speech, of a space of language, the components of which are profoundly social even if they take on purely rhetorical forms.

The advent of this literary space does not only correspond (although these conditions are essential) to the spread of education, or to increasing literacy, or to the technical communication of the written word by the art of printing, or to the creation of a human environment where the written word is of prime importance. It also corresponds to the establishing of a world, symbolic and existential at the same time, where new emotions and living experiences, whether present or future, are combined. This is the 'literary space' which Blanchot has described so well in his book of this title. It is existence itself, the realm of 'words' and of being, in so far as 'being' is transformed into written signs, a world which absorbs and defines man. An ambiguous world also, it makes all the more difficult the rediscovery of the very life it absorbs, and it incorporates all that could shatter it, even violence, into its own substance. Georges Bataille and Antonin Artaud have had profound experience of this ambiguity – that of a world where social space itself has become a space of language and a more or less coherent 'speech'. Is this not true when one imagines that a change of words will produce a 'change of existence'?

The last aesthetic attitude which we can locate in history is the one usually known as *the doctrine of art for art's sake*. Although interpreted in various ways according to the times and to different individuals, it has asserted and clarified itself most in the period when industrial societies were emerging.

Surely an established literary world must exist which integrates and moulds all the elements of the exterior life in order that an aesthetic and ethical attitude, which finds in this 'world' the principle and force behind all reality, can possibly assert itself? On the surface, this attitude to art springs from a determination to detach completely artistic expression from social life. Flaubert's renunciation of the Commune or Stefan Georg's abandonment of contemporary problems, for instance, are incidents which in themselves have less importance than what they signify. What each man searched for were stable, peaceful conditions in which he could work undisturbed. Clearly such detachment, whether it is apparent or real, can be controversial. However, we should realize that such artists were ill at ease in a world divided by class barriers, where commerce invaded everyday life, and where market economy impinged on man's every activity. In most cases, the theorists of art for art's sake are those who struggle against any form of alienation.

Probably no one else has given such a striking interpretation of this attitude than Thomas Mann throughout the whole range of his work; and he develops it in various ways which, as Georg Lukács says, reveal a style of humour peculiar to him.

The last of the Buddenbrooks, for example, is a musician. He is the last heir in a long line of important merchants established in a great port, and the 'bourgeois' impulse in him for practical activity is transformed into a musical talent. The young Henno dedicates his life to art; but more than this, the energy which up until then was directed into material matters, he turns to a totally disinterested pursuit. Moving in quite the opposite direction to Goethe's *Wilhelm Meister*, he finds in the imaginary the principle which governs his entire existence. But his conversion becomes a degradation: Henno is a sick man and the energy he turns towards art is perhaps no longer real. It is the exhaustion of the hereditary line which makes him a musician, and not the Buddenbrooks' energy and collective power which in him have weakened. Is it therefore a true justification? What else, in any case, could he do?

However ambiguous the problem might be, it nevertheless raises the question of dedication to artistic creativity, and it is this question which lies at the centre of the doctrine of art for art's sake. And Thomas Mann dealt with this theme in everything he wrote. The writer in *Death in Venice* discovers a new youthfulness and unsuspected artistic resources at the very moment when he is struck down by an epidemic. The hero in *The Magic Mountain*, Hans Castorp, visits a sanatorium where his brother is under treatment. Castorp's health is good, his prospects as an energetic young engineer are excellent. However, he is attracted and held by some charm about the community of sick people in which art and love seem to be disembodied by the altitude and by phthisis, so that they appear to become more pure than they did on the 'plain'. Gradually the disease gains a hold over him too: while he is discovering love and art, the principle of love and art is being eaten away inside him. It is a sacred mutilation which condemns him to stay on the magic mountain for the rest of his life, a life sacrificed now to strange values which only there appear real.

In *The Mirage*, the theme is treated pathetically: an ageing woman rediscovers youth and falls in love with an adolescent. The whole world is transformed for her, as it was for Hans Castorp in *The Magic Mountain*, and her pursuit of absolute purity in love and art, each engendering the other, brings her to a new knowledge of herself. At the height of exaltation, she transcends herself. But it proves ultimately to be in vain, since her exaltation is only provoked artificially by cancer of the womb. The price of her ecstasy is her own death.

When writing on Nietzsche in *Doctor Faustus*, Thomas Mann returns to this theme and discusses it in much more detail. Does he not suggest that Nietzsche, when a young man, in order to symbolize concretely his absolute commitment to art, deliberately contracted syphilis from a prostitute he met in Cologne? Is not this syphilis, which drove Nietzsche to madness, an outward physical sign of the total sacrifice of his life and of his self-confinement in the literary 'world'? But at the same time, does not this syphilis tear through the tightly woven tissue of words and signs which pervade the world of language, and restore human nature to someone who had been estranged from it?

Extending Thomas Mann's idea, though applying it slightly differently, it is tempting to think that Baudelaire's use of drugs, Artaud's violence and Bataille's eroticism are similar to Nietzsche's syphilis; they are both ways of totally sacrificing their lives as men for the sake of their calling as artists and writers, and also of appealing to a nature which transcends the literary world to which their sacrifice had condemned them. This ambivalence has been experienced by many of the finest contemporary artists.

Going further, one might imagine that those who are in favour of this total sacrifice to artistic creation are un-interested in politics and historical events. But this, surely, is to forget that the most extreme kind of political commit-ment has often come from groups of writers who had previously emphasized the need to devote their lives to creative expression? Where did the first intellectual revolu-tionaries in Russia in 1917 come from? Were not those Surrealists who turned their energies towards politics the very men who had been most ardent in asserting their voca-tion as artists? This contradiction, however, is only super-ficial, for involvement in politics was the fatal disease which enabled them to perforate the tight web surrounding the world of literary speech. To be involved is the supreme manifestation of art for art's sake, just as fatal illness is the price which, according to Thomas Mann, has to be paid for discovering art and love.

It would be absurd to lock these writers in their prison. In *Le temps retrouvé*, Marcel Proust has presented the highest and noblest version of such a man's conversion to art, and of the total sacrifice which such a vocation entails. When he came closest to the experience he wanted to master, he locked himself in his room in the rue Hamelin. None of his contemporaries 'of that time' would have been able to compete with him. Would one not say the same of Musil?

These diverse aesthetic attitudes can be found (except, of course, the last) in every society. They are, at one and the same time, active sources for artistic creation, a principle around which artists can form new groups and ideological justifications. They can therefore sometimes assist artistic creation and sometimes harm it. They are directions taken by man's intelligence as it applies itself to the task of understanding the role of the imaginary and of incorporating it into the framework of collective life.

It should also be realized that industrial societies make it possible for all these attitudes to emerge simultaneously. Never has the life of the imagination been more varied than it is today, ever since the idea of 'beauty' disappeared. However, these attitudes are not sufficient to explain and to understand the drama of artistic creation. It still remains for us to examine the functions and the roles of art in different types of society.

The Social Environment and the Changing Functions of Art

Dilthey describes different and original 'world-views', which are often opposed to each other because they are contemporary, but he does not consider the question of their integration into the framework of actual collective life. He creates an image of sociology which, without being deliberately idealist (he has no use for philosophical and idealist systems), leaves little room for the empirical and diverse forms of real existence. Taking everything into account, does he not regard society as an objectification, a spiritual externalization, a summary of prescriptions and deliberate

95

actions, consciousness and significative emotions? Does he not regard the history of human groups as equivalent to the incarnation of a spiritual development?

This gives to what he calls 'world-views' a subjective character which sometimes contradicts experience, but too often is an adjunct to it, so that one is unable to measure the extent to which they are rooted in society, or even their true significance in the confused triviality of daily life. Also, the very coherence which such a concept implies utterly contradicts reality; and, regardless of the German philosopher's right to undertake such a reconstruction, the internal logic of an incomplete 'world-view' leads to an enclosed monad which ignores the special importance of anomic, and especially atypical or potential facts, which we have described as the 'law of disorder' ('*la règle sans règle*') of artistic experience.

There are two reasons why sociology inevitably establishes *types* of society and accentuates, as much as it can, the discontinuity which distinguishes one type from another. First, such reformations of groups are points of reference which enable us to rationalize the explanation, but not the experience itself (so leaving room for scientific explanation of the irrational); and second, a conceptual classification makes it possible to examine comparable functions, in types of society separated by centuries of history, or by spatial distances which preclude any cultural interaction. The recent discussion of the idea of 'function', of which Malinowski was fond (perhaps too fond), can take on a new significance once it deals with a possible *variety* of functions, or once the function of a phenomenon is no longer understood in terms of a unique finality but in terms of the relativity of its forms.

On the other hand, the fact that these types of society can succeed one another in the same linear progression makes it possible to understand the facts which history cannot take into account, so anxious is it to fill in any discontinuities and to repair any disruptions. As we have already said, creative expression in all its forms discovers a surprising vitality at the moment of transition from one society to another. Art often appears to be connected (in a way that is all the more constant because of the lack of any law governing these transitions) with the change from one type of social experience to another – whether the second replaces the first as a result of a war or conquest (invasions in Europe, the destruction of Carthage by the Romans, Manchurian invasions in China), or whether the change is internal and political (the transition from the Greek city to the Alexandrine empire), or whether the inner dynamism of a society produces, of its own accord, a change in the method of economic production (the appearance of capitalism), or, finally, whether a traditional society undergoes change and finds itself placed in a 'new technological environment' (like the countries of the Third World today). A study of all the great periods of artistic creation, when creativity was at its most intense and most complex, reveals them to have been closely linked to such changes.

This is the point at which one should speak of a 'double frenzy' in artistic creation, to use an idea taken from Bergson: the creative forms connected with the dynamism resulting from radical changes, and the creative forms associated with the exploitation of schemata which are invented during periods of equilibrium and calm. Far from belittling the second, it is necessary to recognize them as being just as valid as the first because, by establishing and systematically making use of creative material, societies or groups can achieve experiences which are just as rich and varied. Racine's art is not inferior to Marlowe's because the latter was at the breaking point between two worlds and looked beyond the experiences of his time, whereas Racine explored well-known subjects and relied on the poetic language and experience of previous generations to provide the elements on which his genius was based. The art of Proust who, with brilliant acuteness, utilized the forms of the novel created before him, is certainly not inferior to that of Daniel Defoe, who was probably the first to give the novel its distinctive technique and forms. These are two examples of an effort which is comparable, but which is differently placed, in regard to collective existence and to the internal activities of social life.

Before going on to examine the varied functions of artistic creation dependent on types of society and on the encounters between these types in history, it is important to remember that this idea of 'type' is not to be confused with that of 'a world-view', and that it is, at the same time, more rich and more complex than this coherent and spiritual vision.

In effect, it is a question both of a conceptual viewpoint, a working framework which limits itself to experience without attempting to replace this experience by a rationalization, and also of a practical viewpoint, a representation belonging to sociology which, either outside or within the period studied by the historian, searches for a more definitive basis which avoids the continuous projection of the spiritual on human events. The 'type' is *a matrix of possibilities*, both subjective and objective, actual and potential, virtual and determined. It includes and animates the different and varied world-views which thereby are enabled to root themselves firmly in collective experience. It enables us both to rediscover correlations which are usually obliterated and to determine the exact nature of certain facts.

Certainly, all typology is arbitrary since it depends on trends in sociology. Nevertheless, the existence of certain incontrovertibly constant factors limits the apparent subjectivity which can intrude. No one can deny the existence of patriarchal societies, nor that this form of life can sometimes be found among the ancient Hebrews and Greeks before the emergence of the city; no one can deny that Islamic, Japanese and European feudalism reveal as many comparable as divergent details; or, finally, that industrial society is a rigidly defined type of society, and that its forms of experience are often comparable, if not in their content, then at least in the functions which they exercise.*

Besides, we have discussed the terminology of these types, in connection with other more complex and more varied terminologies, such as that of Georges Gurvitch.[60] It seems indisputable that a limited number of these types of society would be found at varying temporal and spatial distances *before* the emergence of modern economics and capitalism in Europe, or at least of that accumulation which Jacques Berque strikingly calls 'the modern form of destiny'. These 'types' can be enumerated thus: tribal and clannish societies; magical–religious theocratic societies; patriarchal communities; city-states; feudal societies; centralizing bourgeoisie, liberal societies; and industrial societies. We propose to indicate briefly how what we call artistic creation is invested, in these different types, with diverse functions, so contradictory to each other that it is difficult to speak of a 'universal function of art' as, with a certain complacency, one sometimes does.

Primitive, and particularly Negro, art probably appeared in Europe only at the beginning of the twentieth century. The remarkable works of Carl Einstein [61] and the role played by these figures in contemporary painting and sculpture, from Picasso to Giacometti, show that European man has learnt to see what has lain unnoticed for so long under his very eyes. Malraux quite rightly announced this discovery in *The Voices of Silence*: that a new area of human experience has now been revealed to us. And the studies of Michel Leiris and de Griaule,[62] to mention only French authors, have opened up a world which until now has been concealed from us.[63]

* This idea of 'type' is emphasized because of the misunderstandings which greeted the typology used in my *Sociologie du théâtre*.

And its impact is not lessened, as Georges Balandier states in *Ambiguous Africa*, even if we doubt the validity of this form of 'art', as we are concerned with works whose significance extends far beyond the framework of aesthetics. It is a question of significant forms, whose artistic power we have discovered at the moment when we transported them from the human world where they were created to the world of our museums or of our theories. Without doubt today, there is no lack of African sculptors and painters who want to do artistic work, but they can only turn their backs on that and return to those forms whose function is radically different.

This is not only because its function is exclusively sacred. Possibly this form of art contains a desire to avoid explanation, or the more understandable desire to explain these figures by something other than aesthetics. Indeed, when judging works like the Benin bronzes, a mask from the Congo or from Bas-Sepik (New Guinea), we rank them as secondary from an artistic point of view, because of the changes in aesthetic standards that have occurred in our industrial societies. But we will not understand these forms if we look on them only as *objets d'art*. To understand them and, also, the importance of the creativity they imply, should we not integrate them into the realm of *subconscious communication* from which they have been arbitrarily separated?

It is important to realize that in small societies, where there are few internal distinguishing factors, individuals share, either at an intense or superficial level, certain common symbols. Either during festivals which produce what Durkheim calls 'an effervescent environment', or in the normal, relaxed course of everyday life, the forms which we call 'artistic' suddenly acquire an emotional and affective power. Not only because they appear to concentrate the collective *manna* and to represent, even anecdotally, the social substance which no individual in the society can wholly embody, but also because, above all, they constitute immediately communicable *particles of significations*. These plastic figures are located at the point of intersection between that which signifies and that which is signified; to be more precise, they represent the more or less spontaneous encounter between symbols during the search for symbolic meaning, which can only be realized through the active adhesion of all the participants.

Another major factor is 'that predominance of the whole over relationships with others' in tribal and clannish societies. These forms of communication are the result of what Mauss has called the generalized exchange, the intensive circulation of social substance in the group as a whole. The 'aesthetic' figures are the stages or, more precisely, the *relay-points* of this circulation. It would undoubtedly help us to understand how the communication is transmitted – the transmission being primarily an act of exchange – if we were to apply modern theories of communication. For by the very reason that these exchanges involve a circulation and a reciprocal interplay of mutual gifts and services, they create a certain value. Why should not the imaginary creation of a figure or a form not serve to crystallize this value when in uncreative periods one desires to preserve its efficacy?

If one pursues this analysis further, another element appears which enables us to judge better the function exercised by these figures in 'archaic' societies. In a well-known passage from *The Elementary Forms of the Religious Life*, Durkheim refers to those ideas of genre and of class, the first elements of conceptual thought which, he claims to prove, correspond to the living forms of social organization. 'It is because men have established groups,' he writes, 'that they have been able to group things,' and this explains why the first systems of thought can be compared to the systems of social organization. Thus, the opposition between things which have become signs because of the very fact that they have been adopted by the groups, is similar to the opposition between groups or individuals. 'Society has provided the canvas on which logical thought has been developed.'

Leaving aside the totemic phenomenon to which Durkheim gives an unjustified importance, if we transpose into modern terms an explanation tinged with positivism, it seems that one is presented with an exceptionally important analysis: one which makes the internal dynamism of societies into the creative principle of classifications, seeing in these systems efforts to understand the world, attempts to master the 'cosmos' by a group who in fact remain subject to it. This attempt at magical and illusory conquest of the world by the group, this symbolic socialization of natural forces which society must control through language, so as to guarantee its survival – does not all this spring from the constant determination to make classifications which is present in every illiterate society struggling against the geographical and ecological conditions of an environment?

Can we not, therefore, regard the 'aesthetic' figures of which we are speaking as the crystallization into symbols of these systems of classification, as the highest point in an attempt to create a synthesis where cosmic and social classifications coincide? One can understand, therefore, that these figures constitute a number of attempts by which societies (through the interpretative ability of an individual creative artist, designated by the group according to a procedure which is often similar to that used in the selection of a king, a sorcerer or a blacksmith) represent their own existence, exteriorize or even dramatize a life which is normally overrun or menaced by a constantly hostile 'nature'. One can readily understand how these symbolizations in their complexity, when they are detached from the existential framework of the group in which they were born, remain open significations, *something signified but without significance*, so that the observer of industrial societies, detached from all traditional solidarities, ends by extending them into his art.

In theocratic societies – such as ancient Egypt, India at the time of the Vedas, the kingdoms of the Middle East, the Inca empire or the ancient Mexican civilizations – the illusory value of symbolic expression was even more emphasized. Undoubtedly, this is because of the extraordinary numbers of men and riches ruled over by a sovereign who is identified with God. In every case, one could say that the society places on its frontiers threatening figures, as though to remind men that the world 'beyond' is more real than the social world they inhabit. Comte rightly argued that these types of society were built more for the dead than for the living.

In the case of these societies, the 'beyond' is immediately seen as a fundamental factor in collective life, to the extent that the king-god already belongs to the world of the dead or to eternity. Even the receptivity of human gatherings (especially in societies divided by strictly separated castes which, except for a small privileged group, contain enormous numbers of subjects) is much greater than anywhere else. In fact, the capacity to *interpret* what is signified is much greater than the symbols themselves. It is precisely this which characterizes the incredible illusory power of these figures which man creates and with which he blocks every path into the 'beyond'.

The great ecstatic figures of the Mexican 'pantheon', where cosmic and social classifications are combined, are those in which the system which orders the animal species and the system which defines man blend together in fantastic visions. It has been suggested that these ambiguous and terrifying forms correspond to representations obtained by the use of hallucinogenic drugs, and that these drugs enabled people to create forms comparable to a process which explains the quasi-universality of these figures in the whole of Central America. The two systems undoubtedly combine together as a result of the illusion.

But theocracy also implies a certain kind of state, namely, a strongly defined central power. The symbolic illusion of the people therefore makes the king-god, the representative, appear as someone of cruel majesty or of divine serenity – undoubtedly in a strictly defined style and in a manner in which one dramatizes an existence which should not be shown. The Pharaohs, the kings of Sumer or of Assur, were not, really, human figures at all; but all that man possessed in the way of emotional reserves, all that made him aware of power was concentrated in these figures. In a world where the privacy of man did not exist, where his individual life disappeared, the representation of the king-prince was the most important representation: one projected on to it all that one could not hope to attain or experience, one dramatized, in the illusory immobility of the princes, all that the oppressed man demanded from a higher life.

This explains the splendour of the figures that represent high dignitaries or officials, as in Sumer. They were the intermediaries between omnipotent power and the rest of society, and they enjoyed the privilege of communicating directly with a 'beyond', which is the solid ground on which the entire social edifice rests. When one of these forms (or one of the Chaldean sculptured tableaux) seems to display a naturalistic gentleness, it is only because every now and then man relaxes the exalted power of the intercessor, which the plastic representation gives itself and gives to us.

One would be wrong to under-estimate the considerable importance of the heritage left by these types of society. It is true that Greece does not follow on from theocratic Asian empires, but the sense of purpose which Greece assumed, at the moment when the recently founded city successfully opposed the advancing Persians, was the nervous shock which made possible a new self-awareness, and also un-doubtedly the birth of the theatre. Need we be reminded that the first Greek play was called *The Persians* in which, by a really extraordinary reversal, we are transported into the world of Greece's enemies? The wealth of experience and endeavour, figurative or not, which was accumulated by theocratic societies is undoubtedly, in its disorder, as vast as the wealth of riches accumulated by pillage and conquest.

One sees, therefore, that art in this context – what we call art – has a function as intercessory between society and a transcendent power, which was so strongly manifested as to form the living terrain of the entire hierarchy. Were these then societies which lived head downwards with their feet in the air? Perhaps. But the strength of a civilization does not depend on our value judgements. In this context, the hallucinatory vision of a world 'beyond' gives exceptional life and force to imagined plastic creativity.

No one has ever considered it surprising that literature, in an oral form at least, grew up in the context of patriarchal societies. It was these forms of organization, based on the economic and religious unit of the family, which produced what we call 'epic songs'. Unfortunately, these have been interpreted in so many different ways by archaeologists and linguists that they have lost some of their original meaning.

Certainly, the *Iliad*, the *Odyssey* or the Old Testament reveal a way of life and a use of language which definitely need to be explained, if only because this type of society almost completely ignored plastic art, autonomous dramatic representation or, more generally, all that exteriorized human existence.

Obviously, we only possess a fragment of the evidence we really need. Probably this is because only certain societies which followed on after patriarchal societies possessed a culture in which the written word was used as a means of widespread communication and as an instrument of political domination. However, we should not forget that the 'clerks' of Alexandria completely rewrote the texts of the Greek epics as we know them, to the extent that they concealed the editing which was done before them, in a language in which archaism is perhaps only an archaistic pretension: at a time when pre-Alexandrine Greece was itself an epic dream, how could these men in their libraries have been familiar with the forms of expression which existed nearly twenty centuries earlier? That would be to attribute to them an archaeological interest which is not evident in Alexandrine thought. As to the Bible, is it not important to remember that it is made up of superimposed layers, and that secular interpretations have been deposited there like the sediment of a river?

Nevertheless, the myth of the blind 'bard' or of the 'aede' continues to haunt our memories and also children's books. Obviously, these visions are anecdotal and incomplete in form, even if, as has been suggested, the Homeric poems were the speciality of a school of poets or the variations of a libretto which accompanied the puppet plays performed in the small ports of Asia Minor.

Whatever the case, patriarchal societies seem to have been the setting for a change – a movement from mythological beliefs to human themes or, to put it differently, from traditional classifications to systems of classifications which were strictly human and individual. In effect, the many representations which marked the attempts of groups to socialize cosmic forces tended in patriarchal societies to produce heroic characters, who embody the possibility for man of exercising his authority over society and the natural world.

However, this transition is not a simple one: the gods continually intervene against Hector or against Ulysses, and if they finally capitulate to Ulysses, while Achilles remains subject to divine laws, it is probable that a long period of time elapsed during which men learnt to place less importance on transcendent forms. Ulysses' defence, which is man's defence against the cosmos, was his cunning. Poseidon could play with him as though he was a piece of straw, but Ulysses returned to his native Ithaca and to a human

106

destiny, whereas Achilles ended his life defending an almost divine 'destiny'.

But this is an indication of the essential feature of these societies: the extreme individualization of family groups around a father-landowner-priest figure undoubtedly accentuated the dominance of man over man and the authority which sprang from it; but it also split up the divine presence, breaking it into numerous and diverse manifestations. That this type of society could give rise to a conflict between the father and the eldest son, such as the Bible describes, is as important to us as the fact that these smaller dramas were each time absolute, although they remained always anecdotal.

If in these societies the division of labour is very weak, as weak, in fact, as the accumulation of riches, and everything that established a continuity with the past is heavily emphasized, then this undoubtedly stems from the fact that the poems which we have mentioned incorporate a history which no longer existed. The *Iliad*, the *Odyssey* and the Bible constitute a written memory, a past which is always present, of people who made use of the spoken word (but which was to become a written form for certain privileged sects) in order to maintain their way of life, and to guarantee their survival, a survival that had become all the more necessary since it was embodied in different individuals.

And this undoubtedly dictates the content and significance of these works. Men demanded that these 'songs' should constitute the very framework of collective life, that they should link together the generations and the men who were dispersed by the distance of land or sea. Unquestionably one lives under the eyes of God or the powers of the 'beyond', but these are jealous powers or divinities, directly involved in everyday life, even implicated in complex human intrigues. Epic art does not give to the great phantoms of the 'beyond' the same image that theocratic societies presented, but rather the opposite. There is, in Jehovah's constant intervention, something which is similar to the terrifying divinities of Chaldea or of Mexico, but Jehovah is always a man in his demonstrations of anger and jealousy, resentment or mercy. Is this humanization? No, it is the irretrievable involvement of the 'beyond' in human affairs. Just as Poseidon, the great enemy of Ulysses, schemes with the person he is going to destroy, so Ulysses schemes with the god. And finally, the epic poem centres on the double interplay of men with the gods and of the gods with men.

By involving the gods in their affairs, men were really trying to preserve and protect their way of life. It became a question of preserving, guaranteeing the survival of the familial and domestic unity, and ensuring that change did not endanger their security. From this comes the importance, among the forms of creation, of decorative art which gives a specific weight to the natural weight of objects or techniques (Achilles' shield, the ornamentation of vessels) or even nostalgia for the family, the nucleus of life and happiness (Telemache for Ulysses, the Promised Land for the Jews).

But if art had as its function to preserve and to consolidate man's way of life, one should not forget that it involved, above all, language and the art of the spoken word. Whether or not the Homeric poems were accompanied by acted or mimed drama, or by a shadow- or puppet-theatre, whether or not biblical poems, like the cycle of Pandji at Kekantan, were recited to the movements of transparent forms,[64] it was the spoken word which predominated as the almost unique form of expression. The spoken word was kept alive in the collective or individual memory, the spoken word which could be recorded in writing: after all, these are the religions born in the context of patriarchal civilizations, which also become involved in the epic world of mythical expression, and which have imposed themselves as religions of the book (Judaism, Mohammedanism after the Caliphates). In no other society, except our own, has language exercised a social function as determining as in these patriarchal societies – that of acting as the unifying force for the human community.

With the emergence of the city as an original social form necessitating a way of life unknown before (and which disappears when autonomous cities come into existence), one finds a curious manifestation of artistic activity: creative expression makes the transition from myth to the book.

Myth, such as it was known to all other societies and to those societies in history which existed before the emergence of cities, is a collection of representations – that is obvious. But this collection of representations results from an ardent determination to make classifications, from a deliberate creation of hierarchies which groups impose on the anarchic condition of nature. In itself, myth has never produced a work of art as such – a fact to be remembered when confronted by those who naïvely search in myth for the principle of artistic expression.

These figures we have spoken about (masks, imaginative representations and so on) are located at the meeting point of natural and human classifications, not at the level of myth which has the added implication of a supernatural or sacred dimension. Societies can continue to live out their experience through mythology without ever feeling the need for any other manifestations.

The emergence of the city-state as a new and original form of organization does not, as Lewis Mumford believes, correspond to the establishment of a 'good form' or a stable structure, in harmony with human needs.[65] On the contrary, it must have had all the impact of a scandal or a rape, in the eyes of the world in which it appeared. This should be a further reason for not stringing types of society together, one following another like pearls on the necklace of history.

Because the city emerged from the background of a patriarchal society, itself issuing from a feudal environment, as was the case in Greek cities; because the city became a privileged environment in the heart of a world dominated by firmly established feudal relationships, as was the case in Italy in the *Trecento*; because human activities were concentrated into a confined area and relationships between groups were modified; because violence was replaced by judicial procedure, war by trade and domination by diplomacy – all this meant a profound revolution in people's way of life and their customs. This process was so unique and original that the entire pattern of life belonging to the city hardly ever survived and the free cities died without a future. This was only avoided when a society was able to transform and gather together certain elements of its life, of which literature was the most important.

In the city a vital change took place, the change from myth to literature: to a world with a common belief which revives the collective cohesiveness,[66] literature opposes the world of writing, which requires adherence to the poetic mutilation of traditional terms and forms.[67] This adherence is totally different to that which mythologies imply, since it depends on a provisional or future community – that of people sensitive to poetic imagery, a symbolic scheme all the more different from traditional representation because it suggests a realization which is always deferred. We mean that if in the mythical system the sign has a genuine importance because of the participation of a group, the poetic symbol is more a sign which does not necessarily have a wider meaning. Is it not a question of changes which operate at the level of everyday words, whose usual meaning is altered by poetry, and which as a result acquire an unaccustomed value?

This transformation does not only affect language but also content: the story of Antigone is not a myth because the little princess, who throws a handful of ritual sand on the body of her brother, is merely being obedient to the injunction of a patriarchal rite. Transposed into the setting of the city where the law dominates, where the 'vendetta' like the familial ritual has been forbidden, her gesture becomes dramatic because it belongs to a world which only survives through its 'cultural' exigencies. Is not the poet's stroke of genius (and it is the stroke of genius which justifies Greek tragedy) to interest the spectator in the life and consciousness of a character who has, for the most part, been 'bypassed' by modern life? By this transposition, which consists of dramatizing the opposite of what is dramatic, and which explains why Aeschylus founded the theatre by exciting pity for the conquered enemies of Greece, is it not the very action of this dialectic which could only appear in the context of the city? We realize how great was the extent of the delusion which Nietzsche suffered under, in ascribing to the ancient rural myth a quality it never possessed and in attributing the death of tragedy to the dialectic which had in fact, ever since it first appeared, acted as a stimulus.

A proof *a contrario* of what we are suggesting is provided by the paralysis of the Japanese Nō theatre. Codified by the Zeami school, the Nō theatre remained at the stage which the 'liturgical drama' of ancient Greece probably reached: a ritualized representation of an action without any conflict, in which the manifestation of suffering and joy only result from the pressure of the inevitable on a personified being. The authors of the Nō theatre continued to present this action and, faithful to the esoteric traditions of the sects, never developed these dramatic forms into real drama. For tragedy to take place, is it not necessary that the poet should, through his characters, consciously rebel against an established order? Is it not necessary that one gives to one's own opposite, whether criminal or hero, an awareness which tears itself free and opposes the accepted way of thinking, whether past or present? But the 'respectable Nō theatre' remained just a historical phenomenon. Nothing disrupted it. Respect for its own ideal imprisoned it, so that it never became tragedy.

Need we point out how Greek plastic art also responds to this dialectic? The great sculptured figures are undoubtedly sometimes an eulogy of man, and individual man as well, individualized by his body and his physical bearing. They are also a protest against suffering or 'mortality'. In one way or another, they spring from the determination to place the individual at the centre of human sensibility, to illustrate man by the quality of uniqueness which he possesses. The earlier figures of Asia Minor are idols, whereas Greek statues are characters. In the way they present themselves, they show an artist's determination to make the individual dominate the confused impersonal communities of Asia and the theocratic empires. Undoubtedly, this was an extremely important cultural interaction, since it involved, in the confrontation of the Greeks with the eastern or Egyptian theocratic empires, the only lasting encounter which we really know about: previously, people at war came together only for a brief period, when they engaged in battle. One side would disappear and nothing of the conquered people ever survived. The fact that the Greeks resisted the Persians, the fact that they eradicated any danger and threat from the East without, however, destroying the fundamental basis of the actual theocratic empire, meant that there was a hostile and, at the same time, a friendly confrontation which unquestionably helps to explain the intensity of Greek artistic life. Greece disputed the right of any other human order to exist, and it felt its own life threatened by the enemy. In all Greek plastic art there is a demand for freedom which elevates it beyond mere life-like representation. Perhaps this is why we can speak of art, in the modern sense of the word, in the Greek cities; because there man was fully aware, for the first time, of relating imagination to reality.

One could give comparable examples by thinking of the situation of the free cities in Italy which, from the *Trecento* until the appearance of the 'opportunist' monarchs, were a cradle for ideas, forms and many different insights which still inspire artistic creation.

What matters is precisely that these are free cities or, at least, free in relation to the feudal structures of the time There, life was concentrated, and more importance was placed on forms of communication because of the increase in social density in a small enclosed area. The emergence and development of painting in Venice and Florence have been much discussed. And it is certainly true that the influence of icons, of Christian painting and of varied artistic styles of illumination are not sufficient to explain the widespread emergence of painting there. Wölfflin has studied this question, as have Berenson and Malraux.

It seems, however, that the situation of intense concentration which predominated in the city gave to plastic representation the power of becoming a methodical exploration of a certain space, to the extent that this 'space' had explicitly become 'the actual experience of man'. Such a concentration is the single factor which makes it possible to understand how space could become a privileged concern, in so far as the social density and the excessive communication which this involved made it possible to separate off one element of reality and treat it separately. In what rural district, in what monastery, what château could the space of communication between men consciously become an object of systematic speculation? In what other setting, but the city, could we imagine that the representation of human or sacred themes would depend on imposing coherent patterns on a flat surface and transforming it by making it three-dimensional?

We must also bear in mind the constant competition among the great families in cities like Venice and Florence, the intense interchange of words, emotions, riches, goods and festivals. Into the abstract world of painting was projected the wealth of eastern riches enjoyed by Venice, the extravagance of an existence which, more and more, represented itself in painting or public festivals.

The preoccupations of Alberti, Leonardo and Tintoretto spring from this intense concentration of people, and from the deliberate determination (which is accentuated in another social setting) to deal with the essential experience of man – space – as a theorem to be proved and a hypothesis to be recognized. However, this examination of the actual method of communication within the city, the symbol of conquered and inhabited space, undoubtedly produces an awakening of art as such. In this situation, man also discovered that it was a question of relating the imagination to reality. And, this being so, the development of art corresponded to the search for a definition of man.

One can understand, therefore, that the function of art in cities is both original and striking. It is only there that we can speak of art in the modern sense of the word, because art is really a move towards the imaginary and because the imaginary is an exploration of experience. If he accepts this, the artist discovers the fundamental element which lies at the heart of the existence of cities: collective freedom develops in this setting with an impressive power, it stabilizes and regulates human relationships, by replacing violence with social intercourse or the law, by acknowledging the 'common interest', and by respecting individuals as equals. Art, in this sense, corresponds to this ambitious attempt to organize and develop human experience. It is a deliberate communication, an intensification of communication and participation. Its function is to accentuate and heighten the living bonds between men.

However, things are not as simple as this. As free cities all become tyrannies, art turns away from this richness of communication and puts itself in the service of power. Speculation on space implied the free communication of men as equals in the framework of a free city. Gradually, in the same way that Greek theatre died with the rise of Alexander (who was anxious to preserve it), painting was transformed to serve the grandeur of a prince. It changed its function. Yet it had at least represented a real possibility of establishing, however transiently, a human order where communication took the place of domination.

Contrary to what one might think, and to the idea which the Romantics had of the Middle Ages, feudal societies offered the most rich and the most varied forms of expression, possibilities and alternatives in the functions of imagined creation.

Undoubtedly, to see in these periods only the 'domination of the Church', the end of the ancient world and the coming of the 'dark ages', or more simply the slavery of man's relationships (through vassalage) is to overlook the rich variety of forms connected with this type of society, in all the civilizations and regions of the world in which it has appeared. One could even say that it is the form of society that is richest in contradictions, in competitions and in rivalries – although these rivalries sometimes cancel each other out and so condemn such a society to stagnant inactivity.[68]

In ancient Islam, which from Iran to Spain was one of the richest, most liberal and fertile regions that man has known, in fifteenth-century Japan (Japan of the 'shogounales' struggles), in Europe, in Russia and in certain African (the Congo) or Asiatic (South India) regions, what one calls 'feudal' society has developed extraordinary tensions and, as would be expected, equally different images of artistic expression.

This is not the place to go into an analysis which we have made elsewhere,[69] but it is striking to see how varied and diverse are the images of artistic expression in European feudal society. Sacred expression involved at one and the same time architecture, statuary, illumination and religious drama in an immense enterprise of mystical illusion, all the more intense because the Church which demands universality only controlled certain sectors of economic and social life. Also, there was the mystical art of inter-personal communication, as in the poetry of the *trobar clus* and, as it was developed by Dante, art consciously placed at the service of a transcendent love. There were even the numerous illustrations of daily life where groups or cities searched for an assurance and confirmation of their existence, dramatic performances (spontaneous or formal) in public squares, as in Arras, Flanders and Germany at the time of Hans Sachs. But we must also remember, as Huizinga pointed out in his fine description of this period in *The Waning of the Middle Ages*,[70] the particular and widespread attraction the allegorical use of colours and sounds held among every class of society. This served as a kind of elevated principle of social classification transposed into daily life,* and expressed the same determination to hold the world in the palm of their hands as is revealed in the miniatures and the studies (more plastic than philosophical) of the 'microcosm'.

To sum up, we can say that no other society has so systematically manifested its awareness by the creation of forms, and that no other type of society has offered such intense competition between the rival forms of imagined expression, all deeply rooted in daily life. Certainly, we cannot speak of art as we understand it today, because it does not completely involve the whole being of the person who devotes himself to it; rather, it is a question of a multiple and diverse creation which participates in the constant social, economic and political rivalry characteristic of this type of society. In the same way that the opportunities for freedom to appear in collective life are many and varied (too varied to be truly effective), art also offers an incomparable multiplicity of images.

* In Islam this kind of poetry reached a peak. In Iran, Spain, then later in Maghreb were there not, for example, rooms for keeping various species of birds whose songs, heard together, produced an intense, almost ecstatic enjoyment?

This fact is generally forgotten when the unity of the Middle Ages is discussed, and when a harmonious union is sought in the plastic art which supports the 'power' of a cathedral – for example, its sculptures, its paintings and its stained glass. Once again we can judge the illusion maintained by the idea of a 'world-view' when it claims to impose coherence and unity on forms which are susceptible of very different meanings. If we were to study closely the constituents of European art in the Middle Ages, would we not see profound and radical divergencies between sculpture and architecture, to mention only these two? Is it certain that the art of the builder of Aulnay de Saintonge had the same meaning as that of the sculptor who fashioned the remarkable tympanum over the south door? Do the *Eve* at Autum or the *Homme-cercle* at Vézelay speak the same language as the builder of the church which houses them? Should not a sociology of art have a keen interest in questioning pre-conceived ideas about the unity of an era in order to try to perceive any divergencies of language and intentions, especially when modern criticism explains everything in abstract terms of harmony or of coherent systems?

In no other period of time can we find so striking a variety in the functions exercised by art as we do in feudal societies where the imaginary has been materialized into stone, sounds, colour and words, which try, each in their own way, to formulate a definition of man which no group, no one power could impose on all society. The function of artistic creation during this period is defined through the multiplicity of its forms, through which it implies varied definitions of what man ought to be. It is true that the normative element in this collective framework is particularly accentuated because the multiplicity of communities, groups and solidarities, compared to the apparent unity of faith, creates an ambiguous situation, often tragic, from which man does not emerge unscarred. The normative element, the idealism inherent in the forms of artistic creation, is the result of this tension and of the purely abstract sublimation of a transcendence where the image of man, which it is precisely necessary to express, would be realized. But the whole of this era regarded art as an effort of justification, a risk undertaken by man for the sake of universal values which could not be imposed, considering the diversity of the world itself.

It was, therefore, as if the function of art in feudal societies was understood in the light of this rivalry between diverse and contradictory tendencies; as if this rivalry was the principle and the aim of these forms of expression, and art was defined in proportion to the obstacles which man had to overcome in order to assert an unrealized (and perhaps unattainable) human 'order'. The disturbing grandeur of this art springs from the fact that it always seems to be a postponed victory or the defeat by the absolute.

All the types of society which we have examined are *traditional*, that is to say, one can find their points of attribution at different places in history, without their emergence causing radical disruptions in ways of life and in the possibilities available to groups and to individuals.

But this cannot be said of the societies which we are now going to discuss, because the economic development implied by them (capitalist accumulation, highly advanced technology, industrial growth and so on) provokes, in human relationships and global or local structures, radical changes whose consequences cannot be compared to any caused by traditional societies. The transition from traditional societies to societies influenced by such changes provokes a great many disruptions which have an enormous effect on people's mental and spiritual life. Artistic experience is accordingly among the first to be affected.

We have already pointed out the importance of the concept of anomy in applying sociological analysis to art. We need only recall how most of the problems of artistic creation in modern societies are the result of the effects of anomy: the transition from the traditional feudal societies of the Middle Ages in Europe to monarchical societies, in which capitalism and economic methods of production and of living associated with it emerged, produced shocks and a great many contradictions from which artistic expression drew immediate benefit.

The fact that the first dramatic characters of the Elizabethan theatre were criminals or murderers, the fact that murder predominated as the usual theme throughout the theatre of that time (as well as in the Spanish 'golden age'), presupposes new tendencies which were still individualized and apparently negative, and which were as much protests against an order, as a nostalgic desire for relationships based on values not as yet known. Moreover, the theatre has been one of the privileged forms of this period of disruption, to the extent that the exteriorization of certain human traits, until then regarded as private or masked by the veil of faith, amounted to a public scandal, an audacious exposé of a part of man which until then had been regarded as indecent.

If nudity in painting appears at about the same time in the work of Cranach, Dürer, then the Italians and the French, is this not part of the same revolt (unconscious or otherwise) against original sin, which condemns the body to being nothing but a temporary vehicle for the soul? The erotic protest implied by the detailed painting of Eve or Diana points to the affirmation of the body's earthly existence. This was not so much because the Renaissance, or what we call the Renaissance, had put great value on individualism (an abstraction which does not always correspond to a concrete experience), but because the temptation of the flesh, like the exteriorization of crime on the stage, is an act of protest against the previous 'culture' (in the sense in which modern anthropology uses the word). One does not destroy the system of established values by merely scorning it, but by violating it.

The function of art that is associated with anomy is not the only one that can be found in monarchical societies. Because these societies give rise to a sovereign power which establishes a centralized state and which puts an end to the feudal diversity and dispersion of the Middle Ages, because the most articulate members of a bourgeoisie (until then engaged solely in their trade) enter the royal administration to work for territorial and administrative unity and homogeneity, art also exercises another function: that of being the privileged servant of the centralized power and of the state. In England, France, Italy, Austria and Spain, the monarchs acquired a monopoly of artistic talents which they fetched out of obscurity, from all parts of the nation, and turned to their own profit. For Francis I to have summoned Leonardo da Vinci to France can be seen as an expression of the enormous rivalry between courts and patrons. But for Louis XIV to have turned Versailles and Paris into an administrative centre for artistic production (Académie Française, Comédie Française and so on) shows that royalty had understood that art in all its forms could contribute to the establishment of power and could strengthen the 'cult' surrounding a class or a man who could exemplify the state.

This explains the split that we often find in the lives of dramatists and painters who were alive when these changes were taking place or after they had occurred. Everyone talks about Corneille's 'two careers' without mentioning that the author of *Le Cid* had his creative powers shattered by the emergence of new tastes and means of expression quite different from those prevalent at the time when his first plays appeared. Calderón's career suffered a similar change in taste which, moreover, corresponded to his becoming established at the court and to the creation of plays which one knows as 'baroque'. Many features in painting of this time which appear today as 'fantastic' are the result, as Roger Caillois has shown, of a *rational* composition of elements arranged in an unexpected way because they sometimes conceal a protest against the official vision of art.[71] Georges Bataille has given striking examples of the protest expressed by Poussin's eroticism.[72]

But the 'fantastic' is only a discreet and covert way of registering a protest. Normally art tends to exalt official forms which are no more than 'social controls'. The academic, neo-classical and mannerist styles, and certainly some aspects of the baroque style, in French and Italian monarchies, tend to illustrate the peaceful and secure world on which the monarchies were founded. It is a stable world in which artistic passions are channelled into exalting acceptable and recognized feelings.

Similar to this art of 'justification' is the art of 'confirmation' which has the same function but is directed towards the values of the middle class – just beginning to establish itself as such and to assert its independent role in society. The English theatre, French moralists and political thinkers from Diderot to Rousseau, respond to these exigencies; and the 'birth of the bourgeois spirit', partially analysed by Groethuysen, corresponds to the gradual, often abstract formulation of these aspirations which search for the confirmation of its existence in an ordered vision of life. That the French Revolution did not produce new creative forms unquestionably resulted from the fact singled out by Focillon, that 'revolutions are great inheritors'.[73] But it is also because the only form of expression to emerge in the period 1789–1799 was society's search to find a means of confirming itself – the civic festival. In the civic festival, in the form of a public spectacle, lay the determination to find, through a symbolic exteriorization of the fundamental events of recent history, a public confirmation of a way of life and a certain set of values.

In addition to this dual function of art in monarchical societies, and in liberal societies which, in this respect at least, are no different from their predecessors, there is another function which is generally attributed to the vitality of the middle-classes. We shall not discuss the interpretations put on the novel by Hegel or by Lukács, because it seems to us that the great proliferation of this type of imagined experience in prose form owes its importance, not to the momentary situation of a class, but to the discovery, which remained unresolved, of the existence of a tension between groups in the whole of a society. *Moll Flanders*, *Lady Roxana*, *Le paysan parvenu*, *Marianne*, Julien Sorel and Rastignac do not reflect a determination to be 'bourgeois'; they are the result of a question posed by the writer concerning the multiplicity of possibilities available in a society whose organization remains 'mysterious', according to some, and 'anarchic' according to others.

Georges Gurvitch quotes a passage from Saint-Simon which appears to correspond to this function of artistic expression: 'one of the most important experiments to make with a man is to put him into new social settings . . .' to make him pass through every social class and to place him personally in as many different social situations as possible and even to create for him and for others relationships which did not exist before'.[74] The experimental attraction of examining the real world by making use of the imaginary is striking if we consider that the novel, far from 'reflecting' the values of a class (which was never really aware of them), increases the surprise of belonging to a society where human relations and social situations are multiple. Is not the idea of the individual's reaction to these diverse 'situations' a description in part of what the novel is trying to do? The determination, the ambition to 'get to the top', the desire for power, the Caesarism or the 'opportunism' of the heroes of the European novel, surely all these are questions posed by the novelist about the opportunities for effective action available to a man living in society? The ways and means of freedom, surely, are symbolized in this attempt by a character to master society?

In monarchical societies, then liberal societies, it seems that these three functions exercised by artistic creation sometimes combine and harmonize, and sometimes separate and become sharply distinct. This depends on ideologies, on the importance of attitudes, and on the intensity with which groups or a society respond by their acquiescence or their disapproval to the assertions of art.

One cannot apply the concept of 'industrial society' or that of a 'developed society' generally: it is only valid for a small number of modern *nations*. That traditional or even liberal societies regard countries, where economic growth depends on the maintenance of a social order, as their model and their own inevitable future form, is merely idle speculation. Of all the non-European countries (and naturally because of their civilization, Russia and the United States are European countries) which are moving towards economic and social 'modernity', only Japan has crossed the frontier between the two worlds. In other countries, the *forms* of industrial society have been successfully imposed but not economic growth itself. One can export televisions, plastic goods or films, one can establish a 'new human environment' which entails some conflict with the old society, but one cannot export modern economic production or growth. One can draw up the outlines of an administrative and technical programme, but there is no guarantee that this foundation will, in the long run, produce any real change. Industrial growth, because it constantly expands beyond the limits of the social structure in which it emerged, implies a permanent situation of change, a continuous revolution which corrodes social structures and human relations, no matter how new they are; it multiplies unforeseen situations and new problems to be resolved, and it poses the disturbing and unceasing problem of man's inability to adapt himself to a world which, without consciously willing it, he has created.

We make this distinction to remind ourselves that only those countries where there is a real industrial growth and where this growth produces change (and not just a superficial transition from the traditional to the new) can be considered to exemplify modern societies. It might appear that countries which have been influenced from the outside by technological developments (as secondary effects) experience comparable problems. But this is not so. If analogous situations appear to exist, it is because there has been an arbitrary transition, from one setting to another, of preoccupations which, once transplanted, often become exaggerated out of all proportion or otherwise become simply sterile.

The fact, therefore, that artistic creation *in all its forms* undergoes a radical change in industrial countries is not simply due to the emergence of new techniques for communicating ideas, but is the result of the fact that production itself provokes, and continues to provoke, changes, and this means that change becomes the central preoccupation of man's existence.

It is noticeable that many artists born in under-developed, semi-developed, stagnant or mediocre countries emigrate to parts of the world where artistic creation has been most deeply influenced by change. Already in the last century, the 'road to Paris' taken by provincial artists had become a 'tropism'. The movement increased and became widespread. New York, London and Paris attract artists, not because of any individual characteristic, but because in these cities one is more aware than anywhere else of the new functions exercised by artistic creation in industrial societies.

As soon as we discuss these functions of art in a modern industrial society, it becomes necessary to make three observations which give rise to conflicting questions. The first observation is this: modern society and the technological development associated with it have meant that all known forms of art can be practised simultaneously and have made it possible to juxtapose all the functions of art which have so far been mentioned.

Two questions follow from this. The first was raised by Malraux in *The Voices of Silence*, namely, that due to the techniques of mechanical reproduction, modern man has inherited, and can be aware of, the artistic work of the whole world. But is this 'gallery of the imagination' an ultimate development or a beginning? This question is touched on by Walter Benjamin who claims to show that the techniques of mechanical reproduction re-introduce modern man to fundamental experiences which he had forgotten, and which were obscured by morality and 'culture' in traditional societies – sex, death, passions and so on. Another question then arises: how can man recapture this 'directness', how can he recover a 'nature' from which he has been totally separated?

The second observation refers to the function of artistic creation in industrial societies: the multiplicity of groups which have become the 'consumers' of art has extended the enjoyment of art beyond small privileged circles of fortunate audiences (townspeople or those living near palaces) with the result that the problem of communication has become an essential element in all artistic creation.

We hear endless discussions about the many different audiences reached by the cinema, the theatre, television and painting. The opinions of these audiences are sought by means of surveys which chiefly give information about how certain members of these groups rationalize why they are present at a particular performance. One does not, however, discover how much this need to attend is above all *a desire to participate*, which *at the same time* accentuates all the emotions which belong to the individual's situation in society and also integrates him into a wider human perspective.[75] Two processes are involved: the first serves to enrich a framework of given experience through a creative identification with imagined characters, and the second produces homogeneity, the fading away of distinctive features as a result of identifying with common stereotypes.

But if men outside socio-professional or semi-traditional groups tend to group themselves into *audiences*, this means that imagined creation in this situation is an instrument in the service of an intense communication which it vivifies and accentuates. The essence of art is dispersed in the communication of artistic messages, in the same way that the idea of a single God has been dispersed in the variety of human situations and moral attitudes. It is mistaken to think in terms of 'high' and 'low' culture, as people frequently do, under the pretext that communication does not always convey aesthetic models which are susceptible of strict judgement; it is within the very framework of the intense communications established by modern technology that the work of art succeeds in finding a real value.[76]

The third observation refers to the actual content of artistic expression and to the change that has occurred in the perception of a work of art itself. In the next chapter we shall return to this subject, but here we should remark how much the aesthetic attitude, or, more generally, the way in which the work of art is received and the collective expectation which is implied, have changed. It is clear that this is precisely where the changes brought about by modern techniques will occur. We can state that modern familiarity with 'direct' presentation in the cinema and on television has tended to destroy the differences, until now very acute, between the forms of perception, and in many cases has confused the aesthetic attitude with the fulfilment of the actual historical event. This association of the imaginary object and the real event (obviously perceptible in the theatre, in the cinema, and even in painting and sculpture) can affect the structures of the imagined work by making it more like the confused hotch-potch of everyday life, and by deeply rooting it in existence itself. On the other hand, the television public becomes so accustomed to observing and discovering the world as though it were a dramatic performance that it no longer reacts to events as though they were real.*

But all this characterizes the increasing social involvement of art in real life, the deeper immersion of the imaginary in the existential framework of collective life, at the level of communications which are also symbols of growing intensity, trying to create a generalized communication all the more impossible to attain because social stratification is so much more powerful in industrial societies. Because such barriers have become impassable, on the one hand, the tendency to immerse oneself in a common trivial homogeneity (which at least has the appearance of being universal and commonly accepted) has become much greater; and, on the other hand, the signs which this kind of justification implies have multiplied, so that genuine imagined creation, if it wants to recover its effectiveness, has to resort to new symbols which are more intense or more paradoxical.

* After having received his daily dose of murders, crimes, accidents, catastrophes and wars *in images*, is it not almost impossible for the television viewer to discover what actually occurred?

4 Art Today

It is a commonplace to say that there is a greater difference between industrial societies and societies which preceded them than between the latter and earlier societies, no matter how distant in time. Nevertheless, the developments associated with economic growth and the emergence of a new technological environment have brought about profound changes in most realms of experience. Not the least of these is the transformation which imagined expression has undergone.

The immense variety of groups and classes, the high degree of social mobility, the development of techniques in communication, are not 'conditions' or 'causes'; they are elements of a new human environment in which the imaginary is more deeply rooted than it has ever been before.

We have said that in response to the cry made by Kirilov – confidently asserting that 'God is dead' – comes in all modern societies the cry, no less heartfelt, that 'Art is dead'. Art, as a charismatic and exclusive activity carried out in the nucleus of privileged groups and by an élite, has in effect disappeared. Instead, it has become the aspiration of all kinds of audiences, readers, enthusiasts and public groups which form momentary and changing pseudo-societies.

Because, like all other human activities, it has had to face the law of commercialism in order to survive, art has become a commodity. Although this results in a weakening of human content, it also produces a material enrichment: a successful writer or a well-known playwright lives today as no artist in the past would have dreamed of living.* Success has become the most outstanding problem of cultural life, to the extent that the artist succeeds or fails in 'selling' the work which, in the past, he always dedicated to an important patron in exchange for his material maintenance and security.

Success and failure. This change in ideas has meant at least that the material failure of Rimbaud or the poverty of Van Gogh has produced, a few years after their death, a reaction of gambling on living yet 'unknown' artists. No editor, no gallery director dare admit today to having 'let slip' a talented painter or poet, as much for reasons of the prestige which comes with the venture of 'launching' as for the immense material benefits which accompany success.†

The fact that art has become more and more deeply rooted in economic and social life has certainly invited many different explanations, but they are all inadequate. Because the pressure on artists by the public and the 'consumers' is greater than it has ever been, people have thought that they could discover real aesthetic needs by questioning the 'users'. But this is to confuse the average, and superficial, opinion with genuine attitudes and expectations.

Because the middle-classes in modern countries constitute the most numerous part of the artist's public, people have put forward the idea of a 'lower culture', situated at the level of artistic creation that is least original. But this is

* When the change started to take effect, artists believed in good faith, but not without a certain naïvety that they would become the 'princes of the Renaissance' because they enjoyed a way of life incomparable with that of their predecessors. The follies of someone like D'Annunzio can be partly explained by this fact.

† Socialist countries or countries with an authoritarian economy do not escape from this law which perhaps even accentuates the effects of systematic aid to the arts (especially to the arts which do not involve the written word and of which one can make what one wants) and find, at the end of this change, the problems of commercialism, even if they are controlled by the state.

to be distracted from the real problem, and it is to confuse the effect and the cause, investing a partial evaluation with the importance of a complete explanation.

Similarly, certain sociologists have fastened onto the 'problem of leisure' on the assumption that the working class, having gained shorter working hours after long organized struggles and with the help of technological developments, will probably use their extra time for aesthetic enjoyment. But 'leisure' is not a good word to use in this context. It seems to indicate the desire that culture (in the old sense of the word) should be reserved for those who have always been privileged, and to grant to industrial workers only a semi-awareness of themselves.

Again, because through the development of communication art forms are so widely appreciated, the conclusion has been drawn that values have become generally lower, that common taste is mediocre and that *kitsch* is the accepted norm.* But when we come to analyse the new conditions which affect art, we find no proof that more widespread audiences have lead to a lowering of 'quality' except if, in a very naïve way, one equates high artistic value with a small output of work. In *L'Esprit du Temps*, Edgar Morin has rightly suggested that new techniques of communication, a wider public and the increasing importance of certain stereotypes, far from reducing forms of expression to a dangerous mediocrity, have on the contrary prepared a way for completely new kinds of expression, directly linked to the needs created by this very communication in modern societies.

If, however, we look closely at the involvement of artistic experience in modern society for what it is, without trying to distort it, we see that totally new phenomena are being produced under our very eyes. Some of these phenomena are the outcome of a slow change, others are being formed

* *Kitsch* in Germany before the 1914 war referred to 'bad taste' and also to its forms of expression.

without our being able to point to the exact direction in which they are going or to envisage what new functions of the imaginary will be created.

Industrial society has made it possible for every attitude to be developed, and it has encouraged the emergence – whether or not this has happened simultaneously, whether they are real or potential – of every aesthetic judgement and function of art. One example of this is in the theatre, where developments in lighting effects and the appearance of a director with a special aesthetic creative role have enabled the theatre to restore vitality to dramatic forms, and to encourage ways of participation which in the past had been restricted to a certain type of society. The kind of stage-plan which combines all the numerous locations of a play's action in one stage-area and which, in complete contrast to the Italian box-stage, makes human relations depend on the simultaneous unfolding of the action in different settings, and not on a transcendent 'fate' that determines the action from above – the kind of staging in fact which was the platform on which mystery plays and Spanish and Elizabethan drama were always performed. Yet this disappeared in every European country when the box-stage was adopted as 'the only possible theatrical form'. However, the development of new lighting resources and the social changes which have produced new audiences have caused this form of staging to be revived, and have made it possible to re-read works which had lost their meaning (like some of those of Shakespeare), and these developments have also produced new plays, designed for a different dramatic area from that in which nineteenth-century drama became decadent. Obviously, these are not the only changes that have taken place and, as has already been pointed out, reproduction of plastic works has induced developments just as radical. The emergence of 'primitive' rhythms as developed by black Americans, which became popular in Europe after the 1914–18 war, has never been properly investigated, although it had profound effects on the individual and on human relations in Europe, and more generally, on people in industrial societies. That authoritarian regimes have banned this kind of music, and that pressure from young people, in spite of a long period of restraint, has finally forced them to show it tolerance, is probably proof *a contrario* of the great impact produced by artistic rebellion as kept alive by those social phenomena, the beatnik and the provo. Such rhythms have created sects and these have produced ethics and aesthetics which until now would have been inconceivable.

Another characteristic feature of artistic creation in industrial societies is the change which has taken place in the collective perception of representations of human facts. The cinema and television (particularly the latter), ever since they have become influential, have given a theatrical dimension to human affairs. In other words, the detailed presentation of living history has actually become a factor in the way history is perceived, and this in turn implies an intense dramatization of man's life in the universe.

Not all the consequences of this revolution are fortunate. Accustomed as he is to the sight of catastrophes and cruelties presented every evening on a screen which he himself controls and dominates because of its smallness, the television viewer becomes incapable of reacting either rationally or humanly to real events. At the time of the Dreyfus affair in France, for example, the abstract representation of condemned innocence was sufficient to provoke a reaction of protest from wide sectors of the public. Today, what person would voice opposition to an inhuman political event (brutal repression, the killing of innocent people), just because he has seen it on television?* To a large extent, contemporary history has become a great theatrical event which

* It will be said that the 'horrors of war' have blunted our sensitivity. This may be so, but Nazi and Japanese crimes provoked emotions at the time which it is doubtful would be felt today in the same conditions.

is observed from a distance and in which one can no longer participate except as an enlightened amateur.

But another consequence of this change has produced more interesting effects. Because developments in the theatre have accustomed the spectator's eye to changes which do away with all that was essentially artificial in the Italian theatre, and because the cinema once again created a picture of the world as it is, the general public has now come to regard the work of art as an event which re-enacts the actual event as it originally took place.

This is very obvious in the theatre, amongst those new 'popular' audiences who enjoy a play in so far as it presents real action and who give it an extra dimension by involving themselves in it.[77] Also, the fans of many pop singers look on their idols, not as gods, as is often claimed, but as actors in a drama whose living and, one could say, historical reality they never question. One has only to look at 'pop' magazines to see that 'idols' are talked about in the same language as is normally used for heads of state or for people of historical importance.

But the close relationship between a work of art and an event has other important results, because 'event' means that which is real and unexpected, harsh and unusual, all that is unforeseeable. An event has all the impact created by life, by an object or by a colour. Our lives have been invaded by *events* of this kind, and the widespread influence of 'Pop Art' and 'Op Art', the success of Courrège, of certain non-figurative painting using some of the insights of the Bauhaus, the impregnation of our daily life by signs which directly affect our actions through colours and objective but ill-defined forms, the considerable influence of the gesture in modern photography, in film acting, in painting or in sculpture, in real action at the moment when it is transformed into a sign – all this is predominant in our modern world.

The consequences of such a preoccupation with the 'event' are diverse and are apparent in all realms of life.

Need we be reminded that the 'new novel' describes as 'realism' exactly what we have called an 'event'? In his writings on aesthetics[78] Alain Robbe-Grillet rightly criticizes in the novel a 'humanistic' and 'tragic' vision of man which portrays him in psychological terms, so that what is implicit becomes more important than the direct presentation of an event as it occurs, unobstructed by one man's individual interpretation of it. The idea of describing a scene without allowing the consciousness of a privileged spectator to intervene (an idea whose potential Sartre had already hit upon) is an attempt to make use in literature of the living elements which the cinema can immediately obtain. In this sense, *L'Immortelle* is similar to *Le Voyeur* and *La Maison de Rendez-Vous*, since on different levels both of these try to capture the pure event in plastic terms.

Thus, contemporary literature is moving towards a representation of man based on the event, where the action described is more important than any commentary, and the instantaneous revelation of reality is more important than its description. Such an attempt must end with turning the novel into a screenplay for a film which will never be made and the cinema into an unfolding of an event which never actually occurs.

The theatre has also been influenced by these changes, especially in the search for a pure dramatic language which cannot be used by any other art form, as Beckett and Ionesco have tried to do. Once again, the event, because of its distinct development of action, takes precedence over any kind of psychology or commentary on the action. In this way, the character is reduced to his bare bones, stripped of explanation and presented as he really is.

Taken to its extreme, this tendency leads to what is called the 'happening', the event or action in the process of being realized. As described by J-J. Lebel, the 'happening' is more than a psychological drama; it is the representation of a spontaneous act which is developed and created in the moment of its expression, and in which both spectators and actors participate in the same action of release and revolt.[79]

There is no doubt that these artistic forms are still in their early stages of growth, that they are still undergoing changes whose final forms are difficult to predict. The mistake made by a sociology of art is to forget that artistic expression never repeats past or 'eternal' forms, but always tries to find a way of making use of what appear to be the most 'alien' and least appealing manifestations.

The event which contemporary art focuses on is not only the exalted form of an art which equates the real representation of history with aesthetic representations and which joins life and the imaginary in all aspects of existence; it is also the outcome of a desire which extends beyond the framework of art itself. In so far as the cinema tries to portray facets of our lives which up until now have not been explicit, all other art forms follow its example, the example of what is perhaps the most important medium of our time. What is being revealed by the cinema is its capacity to present to us the simplest elements, yet those most difficult to express, of human relations. What Chekhov or, in our time, Marguerite Duras have tried to say in the theatre, the cinema – from Fellini to Antonioni, from Truffaut to Luntz – achieves, apparently spontaneously, but in actual fact as the result of a long process of development. Films like *L'Avventura, Otto e mezzo, Jules et Jim, Pierrot le Fou* or *Les Coeurs Verts* are not simply films which describe facets of our daily life; they are attempts to transform into something dramatic those elements of daily life which are most difficult to express. And one can see that ever since films like these have appeared, human relationships have gained a complexity which ten or twenty years ago they did not appear to possess.

We are invaded by art, not by signs but by art *transformed into an event*, and which only becomes symbolic in order to suggest momentary forms of participation. Roland Barthes is right to speak of 'mythologies' and of the 'semiology' which, according to him, dominate our age.[80] This is not, however, a question of pure signs, but of dramatic manifestations, expressions of action tending towards the representation of events which is either fragmented or is trying to find its identity. Fashion, dance, singing, all these make use of the 'facts' which bring to history another history, no longer that of the state, but that of the man 'in the street'. And our habits and morals are bound to be affected by this.

And doubly affected, in sexual relations, feelings or passions, because this predominance of the event gains importance as a result of a rediscovery of man's basic requirements, his basic needs, at least in their dramatic form. A certain rhetoric dissolves under our eyes – that which for too long has permeated our feelings and collective representations, so that our affections and our relations with one another were guided more by abstract justifications than by real experience.

But another consequence of the changes which have occurred in industrial societies immediately becomes apparent. To the extent that it is deeply rooted in daily life, art can no longer, in its simplest expression, be presented as mere fiction.

This means that the imagined work is no longer presented in its 'invented' or abstract naïvety, but tends to contain a force which is borrowed or extracted from the most banal and the most trivial reality. We have entered *the age of collage*.

This movement began early and in modest ways. When Barrès, in *Leurs figures*, juxtaposed real people and imagined heroes, he had already outlined a kind of movement which tends to contrast in the same work invented signs with fictitious signs. However, it was with Max Jacob and Appollinaire that this movement achieved its true meaning.

In *Calligrammes* certain poems juxtapose an apparently disparate 'montage' of words taken from newspapers, advertising phrases and slogans, all integrated into the structure of a poetic text. Such forms appeared again in *Poèmes à Lou*, and they are not casual inventions – their deliberateness is all the more confirmed by the fact that, during the same period (around 1912), Braque and Picasso, caught up then in the full swing of the Cubist movement, accentuated the decomposition of the object which they attempted to portray in another way, by reducing their compositions to a two-dimensional flat structure, where a carefully chosen pattern of 'ordinary' objects from everyday life was arranged. Juan Gris extended this form as far as it could go with his '*papiers collés*' in which scraps of tapestry and garlands of faded flowers accompanied 'still-life' subjects.

But the word, 'accompanied', is scarcely apt. It is not simply a question of accompanying but of revealing, by the juxtaposition of real and imagined elements crudely joined together, the importance of an encounter between perception and reality, of confirming what the painter feels about the continuous and persistent strangeness of the world which nevertheless is highly socialized, where the impact of his art depends on its outrageous surprise. Painters of the previous century went to what was still apparently free in nature to seek encounters of this kind. But Manet or Toulouse-Lautrec had already glimpsed the striking beauty which resulted from the clash between the ordinary and the imaginary.

Long before the painters of 1930 gave to collage its decisive importance, long before the arrival of Jean Arp or Magnelli, painting had explored this outrageous juxtaposition which literature, as usual following behind the plastic arts, has as yet only just sensed.

Nevertheless, with Dadaism and Surrealism, there emerges a real metaphysic of such encounters. The unexpected, the unusual and the unforeseen become valued for their own sake, in so far as they enable the artist to violently attack the rigidly enclosed structures of habit and common perception. 'The world is not as it seems' say the Surrealists. And the way of capturing its amazing vivacity is to come upon it like a stranger. When the Surrealists encountered negro art, when Georges Bataille founded the review *Documents*, this new 'aesthetic' reached its climax. Bataille, introducing the review, asserts that 'works of art which are considered to be among the most unappealing, as yet unclassified, and other heretical works, neglected until now, will be the object of studies, as rigorous and scientific as archaeological surveys'. And he himself, in an article in this review, examining the connection between the sun theme in Van Gogh's painting and the ear-cutting episode, achieved an analysis of great depth, inspired by the 'collage' method.

Romantic literature, in spite of its slowness, embarked upon the same path, especially, and understandably, in industrialized countries like the United States. Certainly, the elements taken from apparently the crudest mental reality which one finds in *Ulysses* reveal that Joyce did not think of the problem of the romantic expression of man in different terms. But it is with Dos Passos and the novels of the 'New Deal' period that 'collage' is most fully expressed in the novel. Sartre has mentioned the significance of these encounters between individual history and current events inserted into the thread of the narrative.[81] This is similar to what Picasso and Juan Gris did when they combined the sketched outline of a face with a worn piece of cloth or the silhouette of a body printed on top of press-cuttings. There is also Stravinsky who incorporated into his ballet *Petrushka* a carnival song, 'She had a wooden leg . . .'

We must go further and understand the meaning of what Tzara called the 'hidden poetry' of encounters between the real and the imaginary. A work in which 'collage' has an ethical and surely philosophical importance is undoubtedly

André Breton's *L'amour fou*. In this work of intense poetic beauty, where the whole extent of modern sensibility can be found compressed into a few pages, the technique of 'collage' or, more precisely, 'encounter' is employed. We quote: 'Today again, I want nothing more than to be completely at my own disposal, nothing except this desire to wander around in the hope of meeting everything'; these are meetings with small unusual details, meetings with women, meetings with love which, because it is out of the ordinary and unforeseen, violently disrupts one's existence, meetings with objects which are themselves encounters, where what is useful and what is free combine together.

Certainly, within this poetry of the unforeseeable, we can easily pick out a theme which, in Lautréamont, was formulated in the famous saying: 'As beautiful as the encounter of a sewing-machine and an umbrella on a dissecting table . . '

In this quotation we enter one of the symbolic environments of our time – the environment Baudelaire spoke about when, dedicating his *Spleen de Paris* to Arsène Houssaye, he mentions the poetic language he is trying to create and says that his search was born out of encounters with modern life: 'It is above all in frequenting large cities, it is out of the intermingling of all their innumerable aspects that this obsessive ideal is born . . .'

Since that time, painting, photography and especially the cinema, have illustrated this insight in a surprising way. Who beforehand would have thought (and who outside artistic circles *would* think) of including the most sordid, the most crude or simply the most banal aspects of modern life in an artistic work? The poetry of the suburbs, the juxtaposition of human passion and a landscape of gasworks and factories – this is not the 'leitmotif' of realism but is the essence of the cinema, from the earliest films of Chaplin to René Clair. Is it not surprising that modern sensibility has united these elements, previously never examined, and regarded with disdain by those living a life dominated by sentiment, and which had always needed an idealistic and artificial purity in which to express itself?

If we consider that 'collage' expresses the genius of an era, we should understand that the juxtaposition and confrontation of signs pertaining to social life and signs relevant to emotional experience, hold a seductive and attractive force which is not explained simply by the desire to surprise. When in William Faulkner's *Sanctuary*, an elegant young woman is thrown among bootleggers as a result of a car accident, and when Beckett's theory of the impossibility of communicating is expounded in *Waiting for Godot* through the dialogue of two tramps waiting in a waste land for an improbable passer-by, both authors are using this technique.

Such an encounter between elements belonging to different realms produces a shock, but it also possesses its own creative value, undoubtedly similar to that of the arts we have already mentioned, which combine two kinds of classification in the same structure. What Michel Butor called a 'search for a representation of the United States', *Mobile*, is in the same way an extended 'collage'. What he is trying to capture and re-create is the disjointed nature of American industrial society and the sources of this lack of continuity. Godard's film *Pierrot le Fou* is also built around a 'collage' technique in the sense that in the unfolding of the action – which is the result of an encounter similar to that described in *L'amour fou* – it focuses on elements which are part of our daily life and which we normally consider unimportant. A scene like the cocktail party at the beginning of the film, in which the guests discuss advertising slogans and where a society woman leans against a console, naked, surrounded by clothed, living mannequins whose language, however, is automatic, is the epitome of this technique which combines the familiar and the unfamiliar within the framework of artistic experience.

The event and collage help to clarify the significance of artistic expression in the contemporary industrial world, but they do not define its function. This would be impossible: those actually living in society cannot be aware of the real functions exercised by the activities of that society. Ideologies clarify, to a certain extent, these functions, but this is to anticipate the explanation which only history at a later date can give. Fortunately for us, creativity in a living society does not completely explain itself to us. To be left in doubt is part of our freedom.

Conclusion: The Wager

It has already become apparent that one of the dangers constantly threatening a sociology of art is a static definition of social life. And terms such as 'environment', 'institution' and 'infra-structure' ought to be consigned to museums because they tempt us to think of collective experience as fixed, immobile and similar to the inert matter studied by physicists in the past.

The better our understanding of the fact that there is a permanent relationship, varying according to the social setting, between all the forces at work within the framework of collective life, the deeper our awareness of the existential reality of the work of art. Is not one of the most harmful illusions that of regarding artistic expression as some kind of specialist activity, completely foreign to the reality of current problems? It seems to us, on the contrary, that all artistic creation, on whatever level it takes place and whatever the ideologies used to justify it, is directly linked to that collective freedom which is a vital part of the human condition, which overthrows even the most inert and petrified of structures and which forces human groups (from whom collective representations and classifications are the means by which they achieve integration and immobility) to make changes and to become involved in history.

This relationship is not always perceptible, and it is worth remembering that political revolutions are never periods of aesthetic creativity, but in fact are quite the reverse. However, other more radical changes work themselves out at deeper levels of collective life, and political dramas represent them more or less perfectly. It is these changes, either gradual or sudden, which make possible the decisive alterations during which man experiments with the imaginary.

It is as if the social substance, the *manna*, was acting through artistic activity doubly and dialectically: both as an active determination and at the same time as an appeal, an expectancy, a need for fullness which can never be realized. As an expression of what Georges Gurvitch called 'Promethean' freedom, art tries to develop and expand real living experience; and as something which is frustrated, art involves an irrepressible longing for fulfilment which is expressed through participation. One can say, therefore, that *art prolongs the social dynamism by other means.*

From this one can draw three consequences for an analysis of man, confronted by artistic creativity and at the same time deeply involved in social life: artistic imagination involves a participation which can never be realized; to a large extent it anticipates what is possible experience by drawing on actual experience; and thirdly, it is a wager on the capacity of human beings to invent new relationships and to experience hitherto unknown emotions.

As an unrealizable participation, artistic imagination competes with the very essence of social groups, but it also suggests a total communication in which people attain full awareness of one another, where mutual fulfillment of the social substance takes place, and it is also unceasingly enriched by an intense and continuous interchange. Such a re-grouping, produced by the signs and symbols of art, cannot be compared to any other re-grouping, and because of this such a re-grouping never belongs to any definable reality. The 'public' form transitory groups, pseudo-societies which search for a social framework and dream of complete integration.

This participation is also a way of anticipating man's real experience. The imaginary is sometimes used as a force which leads into the unknown, sometimes as a source of images, sometimes as a game. The imaginary is an existential force which, through symbols and signs, tries to gain possession of the widest experience that man can undergo, and consequently it goes beyond present emotions and evokes emotions of the future.

In his conclusion to *La structure de l'organisme*, Kurt Goldstein contrasts the damaged or sick organism which only seeks self-preservation to the healthy organism which is prepared to undergo new experiences. Health undoubtedly consists in facing up to unknown shocks, in being prepared for danger or in being exposed to unexpected traumas. Perhaps this is the simplest form of human courage. It appears when man, as Goldstein says, 'seeks more than self-preservation'. And he adds: 'this aptitude is inherent in man's being and generally reveals the highest form of biological existence which is freedom'. The application of these suggestions to sociology does not contradict our conclusions.

Because imagined creation is a way of anticipating real experience, it is a hypothesis formulated about what could be, and therefore about the possible nature of the life and experience of groups and individuals. El Greco's paintings anticipated the perception possible to men of his time. No one had perceived his flame-like figures lost in a world where the sky is painted with the same mixture from his palette as the earth, a world which is full of intensity, undoubtedly waiting for the modern painter before it could be understood. The French or Russian novel suggests innumerable unprecedented situations which involve behaviour and emotions never experienced before. It was a young German philosopher who, browsing through bookstalls in Nice and leafing through a novel by Dostoievsky, was to feel the shock of a future which is now so much part of our lives today. Jazz, inspired by an Africa which was transported to America, was to change the sensibilities of three successive generations and make them more capable of discovering the variety of possible emotions in a world of unlimited variety. Mezz Mezzrow or Malcolm Lowry were to anticipate the passions expressed by beatniks in 1966.

One can understand how the work of art is a *wager* on the future elements of life. If our whole being were made accessible to us now, if it were within our grasp, we should undoubtedly project ourselves beyond what now constrains us. But we are insufficient in ourselves. We demand to know the future. At times, the form we give to this longing is taken up by those to whom it is addressed. At times, it has no inheritor. What does it matter? That is something we cannot know in advance. We are as much what we have been as what we are able to imagine.

Notes

Foreword

1   *Art and Alienation* (London, 1967), p. 7.
2   Foreword to *Change at Shebika* (London, 1970).
3   *Pour entrer dans le XXᵉ siecle* (Paris, 1960).
4   *Introduction à la sociologie* (Paris, 1966), p. 173, my translation.
5   *Spectacle et Société* (Paris, 1970), p. 82, my translation.
6   *Le Cinéma ou l'homme imaginaire* (Paris, 1956), p. 56, my translation.
7   *Spectacle et Société*, p. 38, my translation.
8   *Illuminations*, tr. Harry Zohn (London, 1970), pp. 219–253.
9   See particularly *Art and Society* (London, 1936).
10 *Theory of Literature* by René Wellek and Austin Warren (London, 1963), p. 105.
11 See 'Contemporary Cultural Studies: An Approach to the Study of Literature and Society' by Richard Hoggart, in *Contemporary Criticism*, ed. Malcolm Bradbury and David Palmer (London, 1970); *The Social Context of Modern English Literature* by Malcolm Bradbury (Oxford, 1971); and a review of the foregoing by John Holloway, *The Listener* (28 October 1971), pp. 564–566.
12 *The Listener*, 27 January 1972.
13 *Pour une sociologie du roman*, pp. 272 ff.

Chapter One

1   Spengler was responsible for refashioning in Germany this belief in the inevitable decadence of our civilization (bourgeois, one should perhaps add).
2   Paradoxically, this idea appears in Marx's writings, in the Preface to the *Contribution to the Critique of Political*

Economy. This is examined in more detail in my *Sociologie du théâtre*.

3 Durkheim uses all the aspects of this concept, even in *The Elementary Forms of the Religious Life*, tr. J. W. Swain (New York, 1965), where he proposes an explanation for the continuity between different social complexes.

4 Kostas Papaioannou, *Byzantine and Russian Painting*, tr. J. Sondheimer (London, 1968).

5 Peter C. Swann, *Art of China, Korea and Japan* (London, 1963).

6 ibid.

7 *Conversations with Claude Lévi-Strauss*, tr. J. and D. Weightman (London, 1969), pp. 88–9.

8 Kurt Sachs, *Histoire de la danse* (Paris); Abbé Brémond, *Prière et poèsie* (Paris, 1926).

9 'Le symbolisme du forgeron en Afrique', in *Reflets du Monde* (Brussels, 1956).

10 *The Theatre and its Double*, tr. V. Corti (London, 1970), especially the accompanying texts and letters; and *Oeuvres complètes*, vol. iv (Paris, 1964).

11 Jean-Louis Barrault, *Reflections on the Theatre*, tr. B. Wall (London, 1951); Jean Vilar, *De la tradition théâtrale* (Paris, 1963).

12 G. Gurvitch indicates these difficulties in 'Sociology of Marx', in *La vocation actuelle de la sociologie*, II, new ed. (Paris, 1963), pp. 285–8.

Chapter Two

13 C. Lalo, *L'art et la vie sociale*, 3 vols (Paris, 1946).

14 *Social and Cultural Dynamics*, 4 vols (New York, 1937–41), rev. and abridged in one volume by the author (London, 1959).

15 No reference is made to Arnold Hauser's *The Social History of Art*, 4 vols (London, 1969), which, despite its dull title, in fact never deals with the real relationship between art and social experience.

16 *Principles of Art History*, tr. K. Simon (London, 1964); *Renaissance and Baroque* (London, 1964).

17 *Nuovi saggi di estetica* (Bari, 1926).

18 This 'notion' of authenticity has often been used by the writers of N.R.F. The definition proposed here is obviously

different from that put forward by Gide who saw it as an intuitive statement of 'sincerity'. See Y. Belavel, *Le désir de sincérité* (Paris).

19 For a study of 'aesthetics', in so far as they pose certain fundamental problems for a sociology of art, see M. Souriau, 'L'art et la vie sociale', *Cahiers internationaux de sociologie*, v, 1948; and especially Mikel Dufrenne, *Phénoménologie de l'expérience, esthétique* 2nd edn, 2 vols (Paris, 1967). These two studies lay the foundation for an approach which goes beyond accepted thought and is free of the prejudices inherent in traditional aesthetics.

20 *Oeuvres choisies* (Paris, 1959).

21 Lukács, *History and Class Consciousness*, tr. R. Livingstone (London, 1971); *The Historical Novel*, tr. H. and S. Mitchell (London, 1962); *The Meaning of Contemporary Realism*, tr. J. and N. Mander (London, 1963); *Goethe and his Age*, tr. R. Anchor (London, 1968); *Die Theorie des romans*, 3rd ed. (Neuwied, 1965); T. W. Adorno, *Philosophie der neuen musik* (Tubingen, 1949); *Essai sur Wagner*, tr. (Paris); L. Goldmann, *The Hidden God*, tr. P. Thody (London, 1964); *Pour une sociologie du roman* (Paris, 1965). The works of the Warburg Institute have been published in the *Vorträge der Bibliothek Warburg* (1921–31); Erwin Panofsky, *Studies in Iconology* (New York, 1939); P. Francastel, *Peinture et société* (Paris, 1965); *Art et technique aux XIXᵉ et XXᵉ siècles* (Paris, 1956).

22 *Traité de sociologie* (Paris), II, pp. 111–12.

23 Henri Lefebvre has attacked popular forms of Marxism as well as other propositions inspired by a generalized theory of 'alienation', that is to say, the frustration which torments an individual who is deprived of self-fulfilment. It is a pity that Lefebvre has not clarified his method of approach in his systematic series of works, beginning with *Musset* (Paris, 1955), and of which we find evidence in *La somme et la reste*, 2 vols (Paris, 1959): it might have merited a study on its own. This book owes a great deal to his *substantialist* interpretation of Marx.

24 Paris, 1959.

25 This vision of the world is either explicit or implicit, as Lukács describes it in *The Meaning of Contemporary Realism*.

26 An excellent critical study of this development can be found

148

in I. Meyerson's 'Les métamorphoses de l'espace en peinture', in *Journal de psychologie*, iv, 1953.

27 Paris, 1964, p. 420.

28 G. Gurvitch, *The Spectrum of Social Time*, tr. and ed. M. Korenbaum (Dordrecht, 1964).

29 See my *Sociologie du theatre*, pp. 131–45.

30 op. cit., pp. 286–96.

31 A study in *Revue de psychologie concrète*, i, 1929.

32 'It is symbols which presuppose the obstacles, because each kind of symbolism, whatever its nature, presupposes a struggle against obstacles: obstacles to participation and obstacles to expression'. See G. Gurvitch, 'Discussion de signification et fonction des mythes dans la vie et la connaissance politique', in *Cahiers internationaux de sociologie*, xxxiii, 1962, p. 137.

33 *La carrière de Jean Racine* (Paris, 1956).

34 op. cit., Bk II, ch. 3.

35 Durkheim has not always displayed so vigorous a 'monism'. Quite suddenly, it seems, he has come to include in 'the collective consciousness' a sublimated level of reality 'in its own right' which makes his first, suggestive analysis incomprehensible.

36 See C. Lévi-Strauss, *Totemism*, tr. A. Needham (London, 1964).

37 See *Catalogue de l'exposition de Musée des Arts decoratifs* (Paris, 1966).

38 See my 'Klee en Tunisie', in *Carthage*, no. 2, 1965.

39 See Michel Ragon, *L'Aventure de l'art abstrait* (Paris, 1956); *Naissance d'un art nouveau* (Paris, 1963).

40 *Suicide: a Study in Sociology* (London, 1952). See also my *Durkheim* (Paris, 1965).

Chapter Three

41 See Jean Cazeneuve, *Les dieux dansent à Cibola* (Paris, 1957).

42 On this subject see my *Sociologie du théâtre*, pp. 215–55.

43 See *La tradition secrète du Nô*, tr. and with a commentary by René Sieffert (Paris).

44 Preface to *L'univers des formes, I: Sumer* (Paris), p. xliii.

45 Jean Yoyotte, *Dictionnaire de la civilisation égyptienne* (Hazan, 1959).

46   18th dynasty, Thebes, reproduced by R. Boulanger in *La peinture égyptienne et l'Orient* (Paris, 1965).

47   J. Yoyotte, op. cit.

48   Henri Focillon, *The Art of the West in the Middle Ages*, tr. D. King, 2nd ed., 2 vols (London, 1969).

49   For this analysis see my *Sociologie du théâtre*, pp. 73–87.

50   *The Philosophy of Fine Art*, tr. F. P. B. Osmaston, 4 vols (London, 1928).

51   Peter C. Swann, op. cit.

52   Anthony Blunt, *Artistic Theory in Italy, 1450–1600* (Oxford, 1940).

53   P. Francastel, 'Baroque et classicisme: une civilisation', in *Annales*, 1957; P. Charpentrat, *Baroque Architecture* (London, 1967).

54   P. Francastel, 'Les fêtes mythologiques du Quattrocento', in *Revue d'esthétique*, 1952; *Les fêtes de la Renaissance* (Paris, 1951).

55   P. Francastel, *Art et technique aux XIXe et XXe siècles*, op. cit.

56   *The Theatre and its Double*, op. cit.

57   In my *Sociologie du théâtre*, pp. 397–9.

58   This has been analysed with great skill by Charles Morazé in *The Triumph of the Middle Classes* (London, 1966) and Louis Chevalier in *Classes laborieuses, classes dangereuses* (Paris, 1958).

59   I have examined this theme in the second part of *Pour entrer dans le XXe siècle* (Paris, 1960).

60   In *Déterminismes sociaux et liberté humaine* (Paris, 1955). I have defined this point in *Introduction à la sociologie* (Paris).

61   *Negerplastik* (Leipzig, 1915).

62   'Réflexions sur la statuaire religieuse de l'Afrique noire', in *Les religions traditionelles africaines* (Paris); and M. de Griaule, *Arts of the African Native* (London, 1950).

63   The exhibition of 'negro art', organized by U.N.E.S.C.O. and by Senegal and presented on the occasion of the 'Festival of Negro Arts' at Dakar in 1966, then at the Grand-Palais in Paris, achieved a comprehensive collection of these works of art, for which Jean Laude wrote an excellent introduction (*Les arts de l'Afrique noire*).

64   Jeanne Cuisinier, *Le théâtre d'ombres à Kelantan*, 4th ed. (Paris, 1957).

65   *The City in History* (London, 1961); and my article, 'Des villes, pourquoi?', in N.R.F., 1966.

66 Mircea Eliade, *Aspects du mythe* (Paris, 1957).
67 R.-M. Guastalla, *Le mythe et le livre* (Paris ,1940).
68 On this point, see G. Gurvitch, op. cit., pp. 237–50.
69 *Sociologie du théâtre*, pp. 63–145.
70 Tr. F. Hopman (London, 1924).
71 *Au coeur du fantastique* (Paris, 1965).
72 *Les larmes d'Eros* (Paris, 1961).
73 'La Revolution de '89', *Mélanges* (Paris).
74 G. Gurvitch, *C.-H. de Saint-Simon, la physiologie sociale* (Paris, 1965).
75 On this subject, see Edgar Morin, *The Stars* (New York, 1960).
76 See the discussion between Brogan and MacDonald in *Diogenes*, no. 5.

Chapter Four

77 I have analysed these developments in *Sociologie du théâtre*.
78 *Snapshots, and Towards a New Novel*, tr. B. Wright (London, 1966).
79 In *Happening* (Paris, 1966).
80 *Mythologies* (Paris, 1957).
81 *Situations* (London, 1965).

Bibliography

1 THE SOCIOLOGY OF ART

T. Adorno, *Philosophie der neuen musik*, Tubingen, 1949.
—, *Essai sur Wagner*, Paris, 1966.
René Bonnot, 'Sociologie de la musique', in *Traité de sociologie*, II, Paris.
G. Charbonnier (ed.), *Conversations with Claude Lévi-Strauss*, London, 1969.
Jean Duvignaud, *Sociologie du théâtre*, Paris, 1965.
—, *L'acteur, sociologie du comédien*, Paris, 1965.
Pierre Francastel, *Peinture et société*, Paris, 1965.
—, 'Sociologie de l'art', in *Traité de sociologie*, II, Paris.
—, *Art et technique aux XIXe et XXe siècles*, Paris, 1956.
Lucien Goldmann, *The Hidden God*, London, 1964.
—, *Jean Racine dramaturge*, Paris, 1956.
—, *Pour une sociologie du roman*, Paris, 1964.
Henri Lefebvre, *Musset*, Paris, 1955.
—, *Critique de la vie quotidienne*, I, Paris, 1962.
—, *Introduction à la modernité*, Paris, 1962.
Georg Lukács, *History and Class Consciousness*, London, 1971.
—, *The Historical Novel*, New York, 1962.
—, *Goethe and his age*, New York, 1969.
—, *Die theorie des romans*, Neuwied, 1965.
—, *The Meaning of Contemporary Realism*, New York, 1963.
George Mead, *Mind, Self and Society*, Chicago, 1934.
Albert Memmi, 'Sociologie de la littérature', in *Traité de sociologie*, II, Paris.
Ignace Meyerson, *Les fonctions psychologiques et les oeuvres*, Paris, 1948.
Edgar Morin, *Le Cinéma ou l'homme imaginaire*, Paris, 1965.
—, *The Stars*, New York, 1960.
—, *L'esprit du temps*, Paris, 1962.

Georges Balandier, *Ambiguous Africa*, New York, 1966.
Jacques Berque, *The Arabs, their history and future*, London, 1964.
—, *Le Maghreb entre deux guerres*, Paris, 1962.
Roger Caillois, *Le mythe et l'homme*, Paris.
Jean Cazeneuve, *Les rites et la condition humaine*, Paris, 1958.
—, *Les Dieux dansent à Cibola*, Paris, 1957.
Emile Durkheim, *Elementary Forms of the Religious Life*, New York, 1965.
Jean Duvignaud, *Introduction à la sociologie*, Paris, 1960.
Georges Gurvitch, *Déterminismes sociaux et liberté humaine*, Paris, 1963.
Michel Leiris, *La Possession et ses aspects théâtraux chez les Ethiopiens à Gondar*, Paris, 1958.
Margaret Mead, *Sex and Temperament in Three Primitive Societies*, London, 1935.

3 AESTHETICS AND THE HISTORY OF ART

Roger Caillois, *Esthétique généralisée*, Paris, 1962.
—, *Les arts fantastiques*, Paris.
Mikel Dufrenne, *Phénoménologie de l'expérience esthétique*, Paris, 1953.
Pierre Charpentrat, *Baroque Architecture*, London, 1967.
Elie Faure, *History of Art*, London, 1921–30.
Henri Focillon, *The Art of the West in the Middle Ages*, New York, 1969.
—, *L'an mil*, Paris, 1952.
Jean Laude, *Les arts africains*, Paris.
Andre Malraux, *The Voices of Silence*, New York, 1953.
—, *L'art bouddhique*, Paris.
Kostas Papaioannou, *Byzantine and Russian Painting*, London, 1968.
Jean Paris, *Le regard et le miroir*, Paris.
Michel Souriau, 'L'art et la vie sociale', in *Cahiers Internationaux de sociologie*, Paris, 1948.
Peter C. Swann, *Art of China, Korea and Japan*, New York, 1963.
Heinrich Wölfflin, *Principles of Art History*, London, 1964.

In general, the best French studies on art have been published in the 'Skira' series: *L'univers des formes*, Gallimard; *Les sources de la peinture*, Rencontre; 'Idées/Art', Gallimard.

4 Literature

Antonin Artaud, *The Theatre and its Double*, New York, 1958.

Georges Bataille, *Eroticism*, London, 1965.

—, *L'expérience intérieure*, Paris.

Maurice Blanchot, *L'espace littéraire*, Paris, 1955.

André Breton, *Manifestes du surréalisme*, Paris, 1924.

—, *L'amour fou*, Paris, 1966.

Jean Duvignaud, *Pour entrer dans le XXe siècle*, Paris, 1960.

—, *Arland*, Paris, 1962.

R.-M. Guastalla, *Le mythe et le livre*, Paris, 1940.

Michel Leiris, *Brisées*, Paris.

Jean-Paul Sartre, *Situations*, New York, 1965.

—, *Baudelaire*, New York, 1967.

—, *Saint Genet*, New York, 1963.

Hermann Broch, *Création littéraire et connaissance*, Paris.

Index